MW00386646

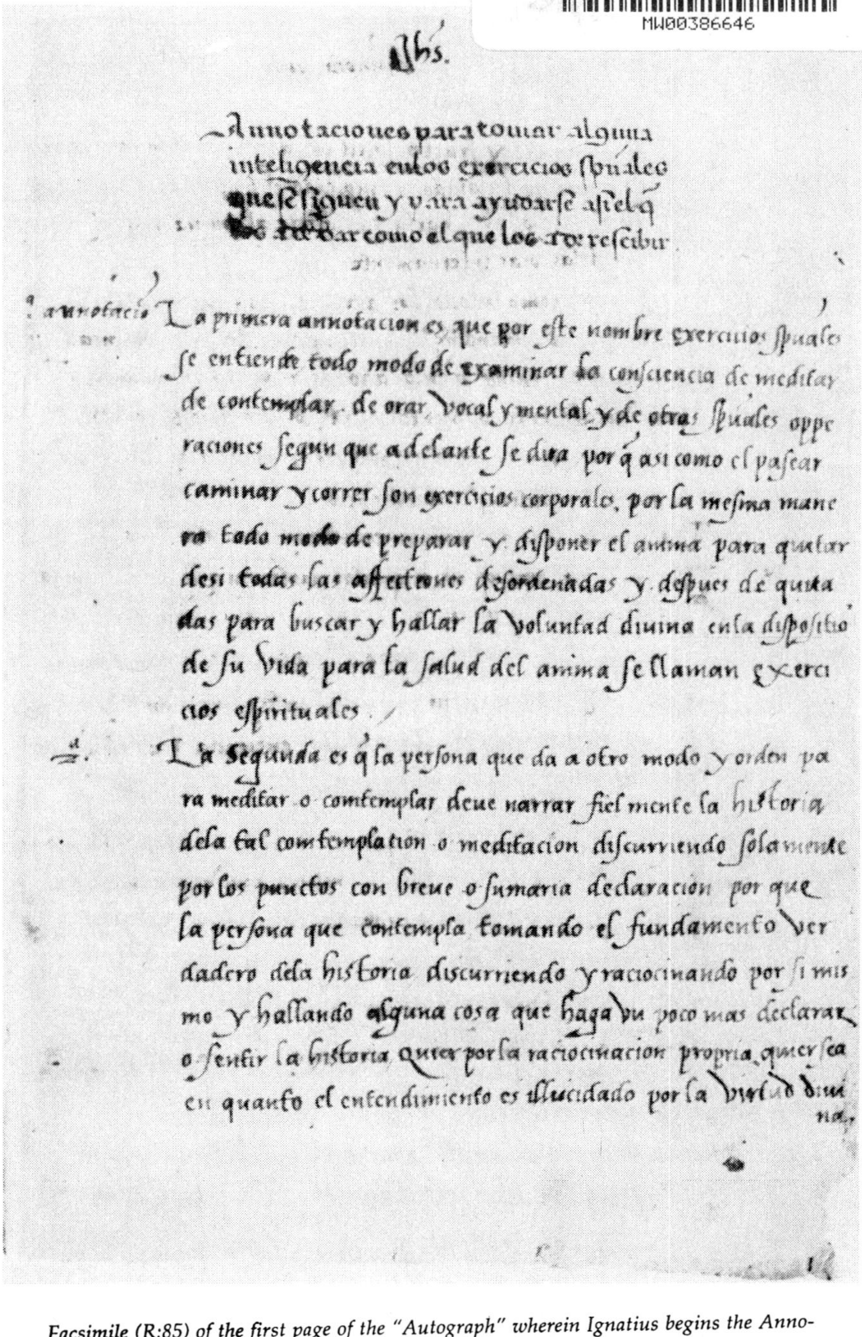

IHS.

Annotaciones para tomar alguna
inteligencia en los exercicios spūales
que se siguen y para ayudarse asi el q
los a de dar como el que los a de rescibir

1ª annotacio La primera annotacion es que por este nombre exercicios spūales
se entiende todo modo de examinar la consciencia, de meditar,
de contemplar, de orar vocal y mental, y de otras spūales ope
raciones segun que adelante se dira. por q asi como el pasear
caminar y correr son exercicios corporales, por la mesma mane
ra todo modo de preparar y disponer el anima para quitar
de si todas las affectiones desordenadas y despues de quita
das para buscar y hallar la voluntad divina en la disposicio
de su vida para la salud del anima se llaman exerci
cios espirituales.

2ª. La segunda es q la persona que da a otro modo y orden pa
ra meditar o contemplar deue narrar fielmente la historia
de la tal contemplation o meditacion discurriendo solamente
por los punctos con breue o sumaria declaracion por que
la persona que contempla tomando el fundamento ver
dadero de la historia discurriendo y raciocinando por si mis
mo y hallando alguna cosa que haga un poco mas declarar
o sentir la historia quier por la raciocinacion propria quier sea
en quanto el entendimiento es illucidado por la virtud divi
na,

Facsimile (R:85) of the first page of the "Autograph" wherein Ignatius begins the Annotations he wrote for the text of "The Spiritual Exercises" to guide both those who "give" and those who "receive" them. Courtesy of the Woodstock Theological Center Library at Georgetown University.

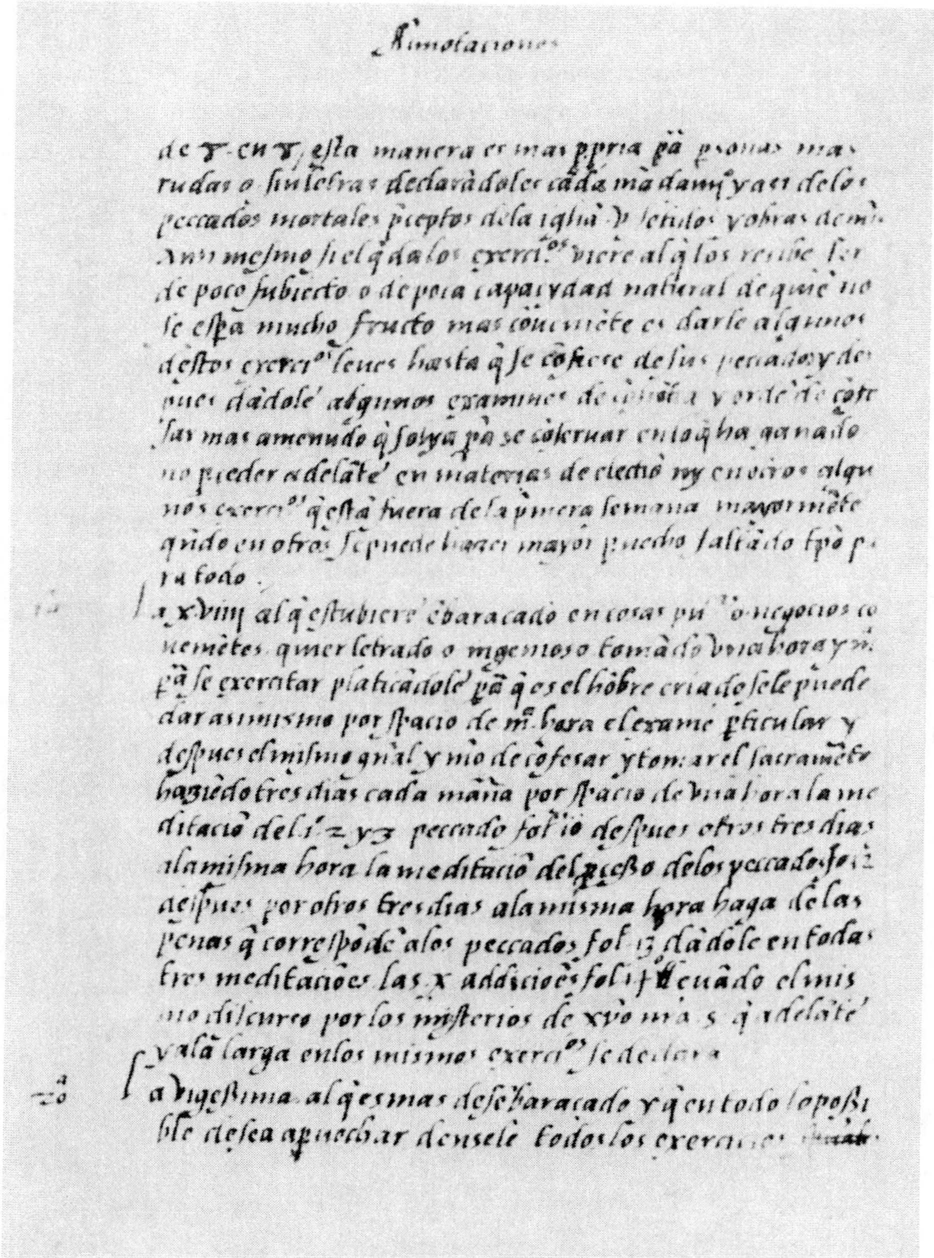
Annotaciones

de x en x, esta manera es mas ppria pa personas mas
rudas o sin letras declarādoles cada mādamiº y asi delos
peccados mortales pceptos dela iglia v sentidos y obras de mi.
Ansi mesmo si el q da los exercicios viere al q los rescibe ser
de poco subiecto o de poca capacidad natural de quie no
se espa mucho fructo mas conuiniēte es darle algunos
destos exercicios leues hasta q se cōfiese de sus peccados y de
pues dādole algunos examines de cōsciēcia y orden de cōfe
sar mas amenudo q solya pa se cōseruar en lo q ha ganado
no pceder adelāte en materias de electiō ny en otros algu
nos exercicios q estā fuera dela pimera semana mayormēte
quādo en otros se puede hazer mayor pvecho faltādo tpō pa
ra todo.

19 La xviiij al q estubiere ēbaraçado en cosas pu.cas o negocios co
nuenientes quier letrado o ingenioso tomādo vna hora y m.
pa se exercitar platicādole pa q es el hōbre criado se le puede
dar asimismo por spacio de m. hora el examen particular y
despues el mismo general y modo de cōfesar y tomar el sacramēto
haziēdo tres dias cada maña por spacio de vna hora la me
ditaciō del 1. 2 y 3 peccado fol 10 despues otros tres dias
a la misma hora la meditaciō del pcesso delos peccados fol 12
despues por otros tres dias a la misma hora haga de las
penas q correspōden a los peccados fol 13 dādole en todas
tres meditaciones las x addiciones fol 15 llevādo el mis
mo discurso por los misterios de xpo q mas adelāte
y a la larga en los mismos exercicios se declara

20 La vigesima al q es mas desēbaraçado y q en todo lo possi
ble desea aprovechar denselē todos los exercicios ...

Facsimile (R:85) of the page in the "Autograph" which bears part of Annotation 18, all of Annotation 19, and the beginning of Annotation 20. Courtesy of the Woodstock Theological Center Library at Georgetown University.

DIRECTOR'S GUIDE TO

Place Me With Your Son THIRD EDITION

Ignatian Spirituality in Everyday Life

GUIDELINES FOR THOSE WHO DIRECT THE SPIRITUAL EXERCISES ARRANGED AS A 24-WEEK RETREAT IN 4 PHASES ACCORDING TO THE 19TH ANNOTATION

JAMES W. SKEHAN, S.J.

GEORGETOWN UNIVERSITY PRESS / WASHINGTON, D.C.

COVER ART: Christ and the High Priest, a full color oil by Georges Rouault, is reproduced in black and white with the kind permission of The Phillips Collection, Washington, D.C.

THE ILLUSTRATIONS: The opening recto of this *Director's Guide* is a reproduction of the opening page of the "Annotaciones" in which Ignatius of Loyola introduces and explains the *Ejercicios Espirituales* he developed and wrote after his Manresa experience. These guidelines or annotations begin the so-called "Autograph" edition of the *Spiritual Exercises* which Bartolome Ferrão copied about 1544 from Ignatius' own, now lost manuscript. (The author not only used the secretary's 1544 copy frequently but he also wrote in it the thirty-two corrections and emendations found on twenty-five of its pages.) This somewhat smudged and well used "Autograph," now in the Society's archives, was photographed, plated, and printed as a "reproducción fototípica del originàl" by Stabilimento Danesi in 1908 at Rome. Two copies are in the Woodstock Theological Center Library at Georgetown University. The title page verso in this *Guide* is a reproduction of the page in the same "Autograph" which bears most of Annotation 18, all of Annotation 19, and the beginning of Annotation 20.

RIGHTS & PERMISSIONS: The following publishers have generously given permission for the use of extended quotations from their copyrighted works: *America* Magazine, Ave Maria Press, Centrum Ignatianum Spiritualitatis, The Confraternity of Christian Doctrine, Darton, Longman, and Todd, Michael Glazier, Harcourt Brace Jovanovich, Harper-Collins, Harper & Row, Image Books, The Institute of Jesuit Sources, The Liturgical Press, Le Jacq Publishing, Macmillan Publishing, Paulist Press, *Review for Religious*, and Sturges Publishing. Relevant page numbers and other bibliographic information may be found on pages 81 and 82, this *Guide*.

SPECIAL THANKS are due Image Books for permission to use "The Expedition," a poem by Anthony de Mello, S.J., from *Wellsprings* (*see* page 78, this *Guide*).

ABOUT THE AUTHOR: James W. Skehan, S.J., is Professor Emeritus and Director Emeritus of the Weston Observatory, Boston College Department of Geology & Geophysics.

Georgetown University Press, Washington, D.C. 20007–1079 U.S.A.
Copyright © 1994 by Georgetown University Press. All rights reserved.
PRINTED IN THE UNITED STATES OF AMERICA
10 9 8 7 6 5 94
THIS VOLUME IS PRINTED ON ACID-FREE ∞ OFFSET BOOK PAPER.

Library of Congress Cataloging-in-Publication Data

Skehan, James W.

Director's guide to text of Place Me With Your Son : Ignatian spirituality in everyday life / James W. Skehan—Rev. & enl. ed. (3rd ed.).

p. cm.

Includes bibliographical references.

ISBN 0-87840-569-0 (paper)

1. Ignatius, of Loyola. Saint. 1491–1556. Exercitia spiritualia.
2. Spiritual exercises. I. Skehan, James W. Place Me with Your Son. II. Title.
BX2179 .L8S56 1991 suppl.
269' .6—dc20 94-10538

To
my first spiritual directors, my late parents,
James William and Mary Effie Coffey Skehan;
and to
those whom I have directed in the Ignatian and Teilhardian retreats,
and who in turn have illumined my path!

CONTENTS

ACKNOWLEDGEMENTS & APPRECIATION

I wish to acknowledge the many Jesuit and Lay colleagues who in one way or another have made this Director's Guide possible, most notably the Exercitants, Directors-in-Training, and Co-Directors, who have engaged these Ignatian Exercises "aerobically" during the past eight years.

My special gratitude to Superiors of the Jesuit Community at Boston College who have opened our home and offered generous hospitality to members of these retreat groups.

I. YOUR PRE-RETREAT AND START-UP WORK AS DIRECTOR

A. Where do you begin in planning for a Nineteenth Annotation or Ignatian Retreat?

1. *The Retreat—how long and when to make?*

The Nineteenth Annotation or Ignatian Retreat may have many formats and be either for a short time (i.e. 5 or 6 weeks) or for a long a time (i.e. 36 weeks), according to the decisions of both director and exercitant, based on the experience, available time, and perceived intensity of desire, on the part of both.

2. *How do you recruit the ready, willing, and able?*

In an academic institution, such as Boston College, the most effective recruitment of exercitants (retreatants) usually results from person-to-person recommendations and one-to-one invitations by those who have been either directors or exercitants. Many potential exercitants, in the early stages of deepening their spirituality, find their way to the Chaplaincy or to the Jesuit Community Center by simply reading posted notices or printed flyers of various available programs, or by working personally with a spiritual director who has already encouraged them to make periodic shorter retreats. Then at the time right for them, this same chaplain or director may suggest the longer retreat as Ignatius outlined it, particularly in the nineteenth annotation to his original instructions for spiritual exercising and experiencing. It is precisely because Ignatius emphasizes personal exercising that I prefer the term, "exercitant," to underscore the "spiritual aerobic" character of the retreat.

As you will recall, Ignatius began writing the *Spiritual Exercises* in the 1520s. Subsequently he polished the text and worked out the first twenty annotations or guidelines as instructions to those responsible for directing and guiding those making these Exercises. The so-called "Autograph" is the earliest known handwritten Spanish text of the *Spiritual Exercises.* While it was not penned by Ignatius, this manuscript, probably copied for him by Bartolome Ferrão about 1544, does bear his handwritten changes. Presumably Ignatius made these thirty-two corrections and emendations as he used the text—until his death in 1556. Translations were also made into Latin, Italian, and French. One literal translation into Latin, apparently made earlier by Ignatius himself, was copied in 1541 and formally approved by Pope Paul III in 1548.

PRE-RETREAT & START-UP WORK AS DIRECTOR

3. ***Who are most likely to be successful exercitants?***

Answers may range from "nearly everyone" to "relatively few and chosen with great selectivity." Annotation **[18]** will guide you as Retreat Director in how to assess and judge those who appear to be ready or not ready to undertake the full twenty-four week Ignatian Retreat. There is, of course, also some need to provide direction to those who, for reasons suggested in that guideline **[18]**, may not be prepared to commit to and proceed beyond Phase 1. Guidance for making the decision as to when a candidate may be ready to move from the work of Annotation **[18]** to that of **[19]** is treated at some length by Tetlow, in "Preparation Days." In that first chapter of his handbook, he provides six weeks of spiritual direction and meditations for the prospective exercitant. (Therein, the term "weeks" designates both calendar weeks and Ignatian weeks or phases.)

In making this decision, you as the director will look especially for those who express a "growing sense of gratitude; sense of belonging to God; some kind of experience of awe, reverence for life and for the universe, being little and loved. Or, if that experience of God has not been so good: desolation, a sense of desiring the unattainable, anger with 'life' which perhaps hides anger with self and with God" As you will see, the foregoing summary precedes a perceptive treatment of the First Week in *Choosing Christ* (Tetlow, 1989, p. 22).

4. ***Which exercitants are likely to be ready for the entire Spiritual Exercises?***

Your selection depends on several factors—factors that may vary from situation to situation. Mainly I try to provide guidance for the very busy director directing the very busy exercitant, for whom the retreat is designed to deepen a personal relation with the Lord as a contemplative in action. Ignatius designed these Exercises to lead each exercitant as far into a relationship of generosity with the Lord as (s)he is prepared to go. Usually this relationship will already have been manifested in some degree by a pattern of prayer, some experience in a retreat setting, and often enough, also, by that person's previous use of guidance from a spiritual director and/or by journaling on a more or less regular basis.

Because of the time involved in directing a proposed Nineteenth Annotation or 24-week retreat (hereafter referred to as the Ignatian Retreat), I endeavor to be very selective. So, I interview prospective exercitants with a view to including in this group only those whom I think likely to be able to complete the full Exercises. For those who as yet have little experience in prayer, or who are truly overburdened (as opposed to being simply busy, very involved, highly committed persons), or who cannot earmark a daily set-aside of one and a half hours for the Exercises and related matters, I suggest that you steer them to a less demanding program with a director who can attend to their needs and schedules. Often these same candidates, after a firm grounding in meditation and spiritual direction later enroll in the full Exercises. The goal of the full Exercises is to gently help the individual to exercise her or himself so as to develop as fully as possible as a "contemplative in action."

5. Why should you prefer to direct the entire program of the Spiritual Exercises?

You may already know why. I know that I prefer to direct a 24-week retreat for the following reasons: (1) because the entire program of the Spiritual Exercises, the equivalent of the 30-day secluded retreat, may be completed by any one who evidences great generosity of spirit; (2) because this extended "prayer exercising" usually offers the busy exercitant a prolonged period of daily spiritual practice during a time when it is appropriate and necessary to *make* that time available for prayer; (3) because scheduling such a retreat of approximately 24-weeks—from late November to early May—is the time during the liturgical year that in a general way best encourages meditations on the Birth of Christ which are to parallel to or near Christmas and those on the Passion, Death and Resurrection of Jesus which are in or near Holy Week and Easter; (4) because holding a retreat at an academic institution during these months usually harmonizes with my own schedule and with that of most exercitants; and (5) finally, and yet foremost, because my motivation is to help prepare an elite corps of "lay Jesuits" to share Ignatian spirituality with others, this kind of retreat seems ideally suited to such an objective. As Retreat Director you may have similar or different reasons for answering these same questions of how long and when and why.

6. What is the most appropriate Ignatian Retreat format?

Several approaches to the direction of the Ignatian Retreat have proven to be successful. One approach is for each exercitant to meet with the director periodically and regularly on a one-to-one basis. The director, of course, determines the frequency of meetings in consultation with and taking into account the perceived needs of each exercitant in the group, as much as is possible.

The format that I ordinarily find most workable means that ten exercitants meet as a group once a week over the 24-week period. As the planning for such retreats evolves I often also include as many as two co-directors and two directors-in-training. These co-directors will have previously made the Exercises in the full 30-day retreat or in an Ignatian (Nineteenth Annotation) Retreat. Commonly they are from among my former exercitants and are thus experienced with the group format I know best. Directors-in-training are commonly junior persons who desire to learn to become directors of the Ignatian Retreat, but who for various reasons, for example because of doctoral studies, may not be able to take on a more time-consuming role for the time being.

The group format, in my experience, works exceptionally well in any environment similar to that in our Jesuit Community at Boston College. The retreat schedule that we use once a week is approximately as follows:

5:10 p.m. Mass (The director, or co-director if a priest, celebrating, the group assisting.)

6:00 p.m. Dinner together—preferably at an informal buffet

6:50 p.m. Group sharing by speaking aloud the life prayer and life experience of the previous week.

This is a heart-experience primarily, and a head-experience secondarily. A most significant distinction, it is especially important because as academicians much of our daily activity is necessarily cerebral rather than cordial—of the heart. Moreover, the prayerful, reflective tone of the group's sharing can be quietly reinforced by beginning and ending these relatively brief sessions with a spoken prayer composed by one of the group. Each one in the group tries in this way to share some aspect of his or her experience in prayer from the previous week, commonly interwoven with a relevant life experience. You will usually find that such a reverential, prayerful atmosphere is conducive to fostering a mutual, non-judgmental acceptance of each individual's account of the experience, or fruit of the experience. Of course, the assurance of confidentiality within the group is important. I have found that having two lighted candles on the table around which we are gathered in subdued lighting, also promotes a kind of relaxed "fireside" environment. Also it has been helpful in emphasizing the prayerful aspect of the sharing to begin and end with the ringing of a Buddhist-type gong-like bell that helps the group to focus. On average this weekly "round table" conversation can be accomplished in about 70 to 80 minutes.

8:20 p.m. Points. A brief preview of and some guidance on the main points of the upcoming week's meditations.

8:30 p.m. Presentation of a prayer exercise. The director explains and presents some point or dynamic of the retreat, for example, either the Christian Insight Meditation (or Examen), or Spiritual Direction, or journaling, or the like.

This last part of the "round table" period is also an opportunity for brief questions or observations by one or the other in the group—especially for those who want to understand some dynamic of the Spiritual Exercises, (usually about 15 to 20 minutes). Occasionally it will be necessary to set aside a full half hour near the end of the evening for presentation of a special topic such as the Election or Discernment of Spirits or the like.

* * *

You will probably try other formats or modifications of the above group format if and when you see that they might provide for fruitful interactions of the exercitants and the Holy Spirit. It is possible also that you may want to scale back these group or individual retreat meetings to once every two or three weeks. However, I much prefer that the group meet weekly, since both frequency and regularity are persistent reminders of everyone's commitment.

Moreover, once the inevitable initial self-consciousness fades, you will find that the weekly group reports on some aspect of the prayer and life experience provide mutual encouragement and steady guidance as well as a variety of perspectives that are generally as different as are the participants. Also, these weekly meetings generally help foster a progressively close-knit, spirit-filled sense of community more nourishing than one can imagine. The 24-week long retreat of almost six months has much built-in flexibility and can be accommodated to the liturgical year very attractively.

7. What written resources do you need?

The most basic resource for an Ignatian Retreat is a good edition of Holy Scripture. Use one whose style and scholarship appeal to you. It is mainly a personal matter. I myself prefer the *New American Bible (NAB) with Revised New Testament*. It has succinct footnotes which elucidate the text and the context most helpfully. You will also need the third edition of *Place Me With Your Son: Ignatian Spirituality in Everyday Life*. This director's manual is keyed to that 1991 edition of *PMWYS* which has complete references to the Annotations or Guidelines as they were worked out by St. Ignatius himself for the Retreat Director. The entire text of these Annotations can be found in Fleming's *The Spiritual Exercises of St. Ignatius: A Literal Translation and a Contemporary Reading.*

In this manual, as in *PMWYS*, I do not presume to try improving upon Ignatius' guidelines, but merely to offer in today's idiom some observations learned from my own experiences of what I perceive to be the full meaning of Ignatius' guidelines for men and women of our day. There is in *PMWYS* some additional guidance for the director as well as for the exercitant on the dynamics of each of the major phases (referred to as "weeks" by Ignatius who was primarily thinking of a condensed period or state of mind within the 30-day retreat). And then you can read commentaries. Today there are so many insightful commentaries on the Spiritual Exercises that if one were to read them all, there would be no time left to pray! I list a few in the manual's back matter.

In the pages that follow I will try to provide you as director of an Ignatian Retreat with a solid framework of guidelines and guidance. I trust that these, together with the text of *PMWYS*, will generally be adequate, but they are by no means exhaustive. If you want more detailed guidance in the ways and means of retreat directing, consult any of the splendid resources listed in "References Cited" in the back matter pages of this manual.

Other important resources you will want are commentaries on Scripture. The ones that I find most helpful on a regular basis are *The Collegeville Bible Commentary* and *The New Jerome Biblical Commentary.* You will also find that *The Documents of Vatican II,* and especially the section entitled "Decree on the Apostolate of the Laity," are most relevant in our times (pp. 489–521). Again, complete bibliographical information is in the back matter.

B. *What do you do during the Retreat?*

As you know, to assist the exercitant to develop herself spiritually, it is necessary to lay a solid foundation for prayer and spiritual direction.* The following preambles and sequels to the prayer itself are basic to developing self-awareness habits that

* I will use feminine and masculine pronouns interchangeably at times.—J.W.S

with time both foster a spirit of prayerfulness and help deepen one's spirituality. Just as, it is necessary to stretch and warm-up one's body as well as to cool down after physical exercise, so is it necessary to use a "warm up" before spiritual exercise and then to reflect on that praying afterwards—to have a "cool-down" time.

WHAT DO YOU DO DURING THE RETREAT?

1. The "Warm Up" Time—Preparation for Prayer.

The preparation for intense, retreat-into-self prayer may take up to fifteen minutes. Essentially it consists of settling on basic attitudes and making basic decisions similar in kind to those preparatory to sustained aerobic exercise. In part also, these warm-up prayer periods consist of a consciously cultivated reverential, receptive attitude that inevitably goes a long way toward establishing desirable rapport and sensitive perceptions.

PMWYS *p. 8*

2. The "Cooling Down" Time—Reflection on Prayer.

The main purpose of such reflection as clearly detailed by Ignatius is to review "the movements of consolation, desolation, fear, anxiety," love, composure, boredom—in other words, the moods that "take over." Reflection on "distractions" especially if they were deep or disturbing will be revealing as well (Annotation [77]). This exercise leads naturally to journaling. Both are important for the exercitant's subsequent sessions with the spiritual director.

PMWYS *p. 9*

3. Journaling—Keeping a journal for Discernment's sake.

In the beginning of the retreat, the Director should emphasize the importance of "journaling." To those who have done it the benefits are obvious; to those not acquainted with the how and why of journal keeping or journaling, stronger motivation may become obvious after some discussion. To some exercitants it may appear a bit presumptuous to write down one's private, prayerful thoughts and trite comments on sources of irritations or trifling activities or insights that delight, annoy, or whatever. But remind each exercitant that the journal is not written for publication but for critical self review so each person can gradually tie together unconnected items from the days' and nights' meditations and activities for purposes of self discernment. From these realistic "look backs," the retreatant will gradually discern certain connecting threads in the apparent tangle of insights that otherwise seem unconnected and random—threads that can most fruitfully be seen in the journal review, and honestly appraised for their value to the whole.

4. One-on-one Spiritual Direction—needed even in groups.

The group format for retreat does not replace the need for one-on-one spiritual direction, but it may reduce the need for as frequent meetings as might otherwise be required. You, as retreat director, will urge each exercitant to also have a spiritual director to consult with regularly, as is common before beginning a retreat. Such a director need not be from the retreat team, although that has inherent advantages since a team member-spiritual director will know at what stage the retreat is at any given time, and will have been a party to the round-table sharing. In addition, the spiritual director, like you, will encourage each exercitant to keep a journal (described later). Commonly journaling is an activity familiar to most who are ready for the full 24-week retreat, but a succinct review can still be helpful.

Two highly recommended books on spiritual direction are *The Practice of Spiritual Direction* by Barry and Connolly, and *God of Surprises* by Hughes,

5. Revisiting the Ignatian Guidelines—important for both director and exercitant.

Even though you may have directed an Ignatian retreat previously, I believe that you will still find it worthwhile to review the introductory material which summarizes the whys and hows of spirituality in everyday life. Such a review will not only refresh your memory but, as is the case with all good learning and teaching, it will also revive your enthusiasm for the subject matter once again. This will be especially true in the light of your increased retreat experience and additional background reading and the spiritual directing you have been doing.

***PMWYS** pp. 1–17*

a. Your role as Retreat Director. The most important of the guidelines in the Exercises, in my view, is Annotation **[15]** in which Ignatius points out to the director that the time of these Exercises is very special, particularly in situations in which serious choices involve one in trying to perceive God's will. Ignatius reminds us that God is truly the director of each person's retreat. Thus your role as "director" is to promote the intimate communication between God and the exercitant, as fully as possible. Note that both the translation by Mullan of the sixteenth-century text of *The Spiritual Exercises* by Ignatius and the parallel twentieth-century *Contemporary Reading* by Fleming (1980) convey the same message basically. But the first is a literal Englishing of the original Spanish and the second is a paraphrase in today's idiom. Drawn as they are from quite different times and cultures, nevertheless, these two renditions help us to grasp the meaning compressed in every word of these simple but profoundly balanced instructions for exercising one's awareness of one's God.

***PMWYS** pp. 3–4*

b. "Holy Listening." Your work as director begins with active and creative listening. You begin with holy listening, as

Episcopalians so aptly describe it. Do this so that you may truly hear what the exercitant is actually saying and so that he may feel free, aware, and encouraged to explore the ways in which God communicates with him. You may wish to encourage the exercitant to meditate on God as a loving and visionary person by referring to Isaiah's very appealing image of the potter who shapes and molds the clay well, providing it be malleable. Help each exercitant keep in mind what each particular "lump of clay" may become in God's "hands" (Is. 45: 7–13). It is important to note that the role of director is not the same as that of confessor. For more specific reminders about directing, see the thoughtful discussion in *Choosing Christ* (Tetlow, 1988, pp. 104–105).

THE KINDS OF PRAYER TO STRESS

C. What are the kinds of prayer to stress?

1. Daily prayer structures and some of the Ignatian methods of prayer.

PMWYS pp. 5–6

Fortunately, over the four centuries since Ignatius wrote the guideline-instructions that are the heart of the *Spiritual Exercises,* many sensitive users have been able to penetrate his apparently dull and sometimes difficult prose and sense the spirit of excitement and adventure in the awkward writing. And by practicing his methods faithfully they have learned from Ignatius how to be contemplatives in action in everyday life. Thus it may help if both the exercitant and you, the director, approach the Exercises as if a bit bemused at the understated way in which Ignatius presents his supremely important message on prayer. Indeed, one exercitants noted recently "how modest and understated God is." What he meant was that we are so used to self-serving advertisers who glorify the inglorious or pedestrian products of our age in extravagant overstatements that we are tempted to believe that only such are of supreme value. Just as God does not advertise extravagantly, so too Ignatius is subtle and understated about prayer in everyday living—and so too we can be. We must reflect quietly in our hearts in order to see God the creator in all creation—especially in our fellow human creatures. John Greenleaf Whittier said much the same to us in his poem "Trees."

2. The celebration of the Mass, including the Eucharist.

PMWYS p. 5

In the context of the retreat formal prayer may take many forms but participation in the Mass is, of course, a supremely important kind. As the Vatican II Document on the Liturgy (No. 7) says so well: "To accomplish so great a work, Christ is always present in His Church, especially in her liturgical celebrations. He is present in the sacrifice of the Mass . . . 'the same one now

PMWYS
pp. 5

offering, through the ministry of priests, who formerly offered himself on the cross,' but especially under the Eucharistic species. . . . He is present in His word, since it is He Himself who speaks when the holy Scriptures are read in the church. He is present, finally, when the Church prays and sings, for He promised: 'Where two or three are gathered together for my sake, there am I in the midst of them'" (Mt. 18:20).

3. Meditation or "prayer of the Heart."

PMWYS
pp. 6–9

PMWYS
pp. 9–10

The meditation period which commonly is energized by and often follows formal prayer is central to the retreatant's goal of devoting one and one-half hours to spiritual exercises each day of the retreat. Although not itself formal prayer, this reflection on, or a review of, what has happened during the formal prayer period is very important. In his instructions, Ignatius recommends that each exercitant keep a journal that will record some of the words and pictures that flow into one's natural reflections or awareness of one's self. This "look back" is the so-called "discernment of the spirits" which enter our innermost stream of consciousness during the prayer period. The journal will be very helpful for reviewing reflectively the highlights on the path thus walked and for taking note of patterns that are inevitably revealed. As director of these Exercises, you will also want to stress that if the exercitant does not journal, it is unlikely that he will become sensitive to and aware of the pattern of graced gifts that often come into one's life. Recall also, a journal serves to remind an exercitant of points that he may wish to bring up during meetings with his spiritual director.

4. Focus on the "Heart" is primary in meditation.

Emphasize to the group that meditation is primarily actions of the heart—the affections, that is—not principally actions of the head. Ignatius recognized that reading and thinking about what we would now call aerobic exercises is a world apart from engaging in them. Many of us who are involved in academic pursuits, tend mistakenly to carry over habits of study to our prayer. The practice of spirituality is dominantly a habit of the heart that must be cultivated in much the same way as falling deeply in love with a good person or a good occupation to whom or to which we can give of all that we are or of all that we aspire to. Spirituality is not primarily an intellectual pursuit, yet it is not anti-intellectual, and it may be aided by theological study and other intellection. But it is an exercise for and of the heart, even as aerobic exercises are in the realm of physical fitness. Indeed, eventually as a director you will find yourself training each retreatant to focus all emotional energy into the act of placing his whole self in the presence and service of God.

When I first encountered the late Tony de Mello, S.J., he asked us exercitants to leave academic approaches at the door as it were and to engage our hearts instead. I must admit I was disappointed that a fellow Jesuit with strong academic training should have so little regard for the supremacy of the intellect. But that retreat, based largely on Buddhist-Christian methods that emphasize non-cerebral focusing and Eastern meditation practice, changed the course of my life. In a paradoxical twist it not only gave me a proper basis for Ignatian spirituality but also grounded my academic endeavors more firmly. I believe that Ignatian spirituality presupposes many of the principles that are such a prominent part of Buddhist spiritual practice, such as awareness meditation. I suggest that you read over "A Buddhist-Christian Method of Prayer" because it is a practical way to work toward interior silence, focusing, and discernment.

THE KINDS OF PRAYER TO STRESS

PMWYS *pp. 19–20*

In 1930 and 1932, John Macmurray in a series of broadcast lectures, analyzed the worldwide crisis in society of that time as a loss of faith. To him, faith was not principally "an intellectual assent to truths, but a heartfelt commitment to transcendent values and to God's intention for our world." That "distant early warning" is cited in *Now Choose Life* (Barry, 1990, p. 21). Macmurray reminds us that while there has been an extraordinary development of knowledge since the breakup of the medieval world, "there has been no corresponding emotional development. As a result we are intellectually civilized" but . . . "emotionally we are primitive, childish, undeveloped."

"Macmurray saw that we must cultivate our emotions or lose the very freedom of thought we prize so much . . . He maintains, therefore, that our emotions can become as rational, as attuned to reality, as our intellects. (He) claims that a disciplined testing of our emotions will uncover their inner rationality; will, indeed, uncover the laws imprinted in our hearts by the Creator . . . I believe that what Ignatius of Loyola calls the discernment of spirits aims at just such a disciplined testing of our feelings, our emotions, our values, our hearts . . . if we want to address the spiritual and moral crisis of our times, all of us, and especially spiritual leaders, will have to challenge ourselves to engage in the discernment of spirits" (Barry, 1990, pp. 23–25).

5. Awareness Examen, the Examen of Consciousness, or the Christian Insight Meditation (CIM).

Ignatius attached great importance to a simple, daily review of the ways in which God is present in one's life. Sometimes termed "self examination," what he called the Examen, has become over time a term overloaded with sterile baggage. And so I attempt to modify it, first of all by referring to it as Insight

Meditation, so as to emphasize its positive features, because it has been so often misunderstood as preoccupation with self. Ignatius felt that the spirit of awareness should pervade one's entire day and for that, an examen or honest reappraisal, should be a short period of formal prayer, up to 15 minutes in length and preferably twice a day. Each such "look back" period should be a time to pray for enlightenment, to give quiet thanks for the fruits received since the last Examen, and then to gratefully review the day for practical signs of God's presence and gifts. And finally to be optimistically contrite and joyous as one looks forward to the next period of prayer.

PMWYS *pp. 10–12*

The Awareness Examen is basically a meditative way of throwing off your shoes at the end of the day, relaxing in God's embrace, with gratitude for all of the many ways, joyous or painful, in which God has been present to you this day. This gratitude will overflow into the question, "What have I done for God today? What ought I to do in return for all that God has done for me? Ever? This day? Overwhelmed by God's presence, it is only natural, as well as supernatural, that I should this day and each day leave my baggage of sin and weakness behind. Then I may go forward upheld by God's strength and healed, or in the process of healing, from wounds inflicted by the slings and arrows of God's enemy, and proceed with a lighter load.

This is the most important meditative activity prescribed in the *Spiritual Exercises.* No matter what other kind of exercise must be omitted for whatever reason, this Awareness Meditation should never be abandoned. Used as intended originally, the Examen or CIM (my term) can become a delightful and consoling source of spiritual strength.

6. Praying the poems or "songs of the Heart"

The poems or "songs of the heart" offered in *Place Me With Your Son* at the close of each week's meditations are especially meant to help us capture the spirit of some aspect of the evolving retreat experience. I have discovered that most exercitants find these and the other poems and prayers, like Ignatius' own, nearly always express some of the deep feelings they are experiencing and may often be the "breath of life" that can energize the quadruple colloquy. Thus, for the many who react positively, the works of these various good poets are a resource of great value in the movement toward contemplation. This third edition of *PMWYS* is the beneficiary of the excellent and appropriate poems chosen by the editors of the earlier editions. They are all Jesuits of the Maryland Province, who are named on the Permissions page in the front matter of the book.

II. WHAT IS "THE SPIRITUAL EXERCISES"? AND WHAT ARE SPIRITUAL EXERCISES?

A. The Text of, the Translations of, and the Commentaries on "The Spiritual Exercises"

1. Ignatius' own definition and explanation.

An eminently sensible and efficient answer to the questions above was written at the very beginning by the author of *The Spiritual Exercises*:

After his first words, a dedication and the caption "**IHS, ANNOTATIONS**, the Autograph continues:

"TO GIVE SOME UNDERSTANDING OF THE
SPIRITUAL EXERCISES WHICH FOLLOW,
AND TO ENABLE HIM WHO IS TO GIVE
AND HIM WHO IS TO RECEIVE THEM
TO HELP THEMSELVES."

Then Ignatius expands on his concepts in terms meant to appeal to active, concerned people bent on managing their lives well. And Mullan, in his careful English, captured the essence of that history-making, practical first instruction:

> **First Annotation.** The first Annotation is that by this name of Spiritual Exercises is meant every way of examining one's conscience, of meditating, of contemplating, of praying vocally and mentally, and of performing other spiritual actions, as will be said later. For as strolling, walking and running are bodily exercises, so every way of preparing and disposing the soul to rid itself of all the disordered tendencies, and after it is rid, to seek and find the Divine Will as to the management of one's life for the salvation of the soul, is called Spiritual Exercise (Fleming, 1978, p. 4).

If Ignatius were writing today he might have called the above exercises "Spiritual Aerobics" so as to better convey to us as people of action the idea that personal exertion is required for spiritual benefits just as it is for good physical well being. It will be instructive for the exercitant to refer again to that text as taken literally from the Spanish and then as paraphrased **[1]**. (Fleming, 1978, p. 5). Even in this edition, *The Spiritual Exercises* are so succinct and so apparently prosaic that their style all too readily hides the depth of mystical insight that Ignatius brought to their composition. Indeed Harvey Egan points out "that Ignatius was an incomparable mystic whose mystical and apostolic gifts are really two sides of the same coin. Ignatius was apostolic *because* he was one of the greatest mystics the Church has ever seen. His apostolic successes are the mystical expressions, the sacramental embodiment, of his radical mysticism."

In the words of Alfred Feder, one of many twentieth-century Ignatian scholars, Ignatius of Loyola was a "man of the most penetrating intellect, immense strength of will and untiring energy, averse to all fanaticism and fantasy, filled with the *purest love of God and neighbor.*" Agreeing with Feder, Egan goes on to say that "Ignatius' decisive influence in the world and church history flows from his *mystical* love of God and neighbor. His mystical purification by, illumination by, and union with the God who so loved the world remains the definitive horizon within which *everything* said about him must be considered."(Egan, 1987, p. 19; *emphasis* added).

2. *The original text and translations of "The Spiritual Exercises."*

PMWYS *pp. 4*

The text of The Spiritual Exercises by Ignatius, referred to by Fleming as *The Literal Translation,* is just that, a word for word translation made by Elder Mullan, S.J., in 1909 from the original Spanish of Ignatius. Although designated the Autograph, it is not in the handwriting of Ignatius, but it does contain a number of hand-written corrections made by Ignatius and it was used by him in presenting the Exercises. This surviving manuscript was selected for translation by Mullan because of its "accuracy in reproducing Ignatius' thought, nuances, and style." (Fleming, 1978, p. xiv). Originally Ignatius organized the text as a series of numbered Annotations or as we might say, Guidelines, in order that a director as well as an exercitant would have help making the Exercises. To designate such an Annotation in the Fleming edition, this manual uses a bold number in bold square brackets **[19]**. (As an aside, Elder Mullan was a scholarly luminary of the Maryland Province.)

The text as written by Ignatius is a difficult one and, because it is organized in such a succinct and matter of fact, step-by-step cook book style, "its real secret—its mystical foundation" has often been overlooked by many sophisticated, style-conscious readers. "Some contend that the Exercises teach only highly discursive, image-bound, and somewhat mechanical methods of prayer, suitable only for beginners and an actual barrier to deeper, more mystical levels of prayer. . . . Yet as one of the foremost writers on mysticism, Evelyn Underhill, points out, 'the concrete nature of St. Ignatius' work, especially its later developments, has blinded historians to the fact that he was a true mystic.'" (Egan, 1987, pp. 18–19).

3. Selected Commentaries on "The Spiritual Exercises."

There are many excellent commentaries on the complete text of *The Spiritual Exercises* and on selected aspects of them. Several excellent books on spiritual direction are also available as well as a plethora of relatively recent studies on various methods of prayer including the Ignatian forms. Your choice of supplementary reading of commentaries is, in part, a matter of preference and experience, as well as of considerations of time and energy.

In addition to commentaries noted earlier in this manual (Part I—"Your Pre-Retreat and Start-up Work as Director"), the works of the following authors are to be found in the back matter under References. These, who have been most useful for my purposes, include: Gilles Cusson, Gerard W. Hughes, David M. Stanley, Jules Toner, and Harvey D. Egan, translator of Rahner's *The Theologian*.

Another contemporary student of the *Exercises* and of spiritual direction whose prolific writings "ignite" the heart of his readers is William Barry, S.J. He imparts insightful warmth in anecdotes and stories that illustrate how the principles of the *Spiritual Exercises* have been lived out and by appealing to and emotionally engaging us with credible persons and situations. Examples of Barry's writings are all cited in the back matter. His sensitive writings will nourish the reader with a penetrating look at what Ignatius intended and his powerful explication of the dynamics of the *Exercises* is also vivid and emotional.

B. Fundamental Insights into the Mysticism of the Spiritual Exercises

1. Ignatian Mysticism or Spirituality is preeminently Trinitarian.

In order to approach the retreat from the same frame of reference that Ignatius used when he developed these Exercises the exercitant should to be aware throughout that the mysticism or spirituality of that sixteenth-century writer is preeminently trinitarian. As the director you should be sure that the trinitarian perspective is emphasized frequently and explicitly throughout the retreat. The brief citations I use from *Ignatius Loyola the Mystic* should be supplemented by a more thorough reading on the topic from that excellent study and from sources that he cites (Egan, 1987, pp. 66–118).

"Because Ignatius attained the fullness of Christian life, the perfection of the life of faith, hope, and love, he was a mystic, and vice versa. The triune God purified, illuminated, and transformed Ignatius. The Trinity bestowed upon him full participation in its life, especially through Ignatius' radical imitation of Christ's life, death and resurrection. The triune God called Ignatius to the very depths of his spirit and beyond all narcissistic introversion to share fully in the divine life. Ignatius courageously risked everything and surrendered totally to the Trinity. And the more deeply God united Ignatius to the inner-trinitarian life, the more deeply God united him to others in loving service to the entire world. What began in his very depths compelled Ignatius to communicate it to all dimensions of human existence."

"Thus, Ignatius' mysticism is first and foremost explicitly, trinitarian. But it is likewise Christ-centered, eucharistic, and priestly. Mediators, such as the Virgin Mary, the angels, the entire heavenly court, and so on, were also important for his mystical life. Ignatius found God in all things and all things in God. Karl Rahner speaks of this as a 'mysticism of joy in the world.'" (Egan, 1987, pp. 19–20).

This view of Ignatius' Spirit-centered mysticism is further explained: "Constantly in communication with the triune God, Ignatius received gifts from each person corresponding to that person's nature. That is, he experienced not only 'God' or the 'Trinity,' but more specifically the Father *as* Father, the Son *as* Son, and the Holy Spirit *as* Holy Spirit . . . The trinitarian experiences at Manresa enabled Ignatius to find the Trinity in all things and all things in the Trinity." Hence, "creation, salvation history, God's gifts to the person, and the like—as depicted in the *Spiritual Exercises*—can only be grasped within their trinitarian perspective. . . ." (Egan, 1987, p. 67).

Moreover, the two small packets of notes known as Ignatius' *Spiritual Diary* are regarded as "perhaps the most remarkable document on trinitarian mysticism ever written in any language."(Egan, 1987, p. 68). Again, Egan reminds us that his "mystical devotion, or 'ease in finding God,' was often directed toward and terminated in the Trinity or a person of the Trinity. [Ignatius] had little difficulty attaining devotion, although he says explicitly that he still had to prepare for it and that it was not always given (Egan, 1987, p. 69).

FUNDAMENTAL INSIGHTS INTO THE MYSTICISM OF THE EXERCISES

2. *Ignatian Mysticism knows the Father as Father.*

As we are further reminded: "Ignatius mystically experienced the Father as Father." Ignatius' response to the statement of the Father at La Storta was such that it transformed his heart: "'I shall be favorable to you [plural] at Rome' Moreover, when the eternal Father and his cross-bearing Son appeared to Ignatius, it is again the Father who says to Christ, 'I want you to take this man as your servant.'" And Ignatius understood Christ's reply to be, "'I want you [Ignatius] to serve us [Father and Christ].'" (Egan, 1987, p. 77). From the foregoing passages Egan concludes that the explicitly Father-centered aspect of Ignatian mysticism cannot be denied.

"Although the *Spiritual Exercises* focus for the most part on the life, death, and resurrection of Jesus Christ, nonetheless the eternal Father is still their all-embracing horizon. For Jesus Christ is essentially the one sent by the Father to accomplish his will" (Egan, 1987, p.80). Numerous citations throughout the *Exercises* refer to the Father. In the contemplation on Christ the King and his Call in Week 5, of Phase One, Ignatius hears Jesus say: "It is my will to conquer all the world and all enemies and so to enter into the glory of My Father" **[95]**. It is clear that some of the most important graces and consolations of Phase One of the Exercises are only the Father's to give **[63]** and that "the eternal Father is perhaps the key figure in the frequently repeated and highly important Quadruple* Colloquy, in which the exercitant asks Mary, then Christ, the Holy Spirit, and then the Father for certain graces" (Egan, 1987, p. 80).

PMWYS *pp. 49–52*

In the meditation on Two Leaders and Two Strategies in Week 9 of Phase Two it is immediately clear in the First Colloquy that the exercitant must ask this grace from the Father and from mediators **[147–148]**. Further clarification can be found in the third edition considerations. A number of meditations and contemplations in *The Spiritual Exercises* focus on Jesus "praying to his Father **[201, 290]**, being about his Father's business **[272]**, being called the Father's beloved Son **[273]**, driving the sellers from his Father's house **[277]**, telling his followers to give glory

PMWYS *pp. 77–82*

* Traditionally called the "Triple Colloquy," but re-titled by me since I agree with the numerous Ignatian scholars who think that the Holy Spirit was only not explicitly identified here by Ignatius in deference to those in the Church who vehemently deplored the excesses then current among many adherents of a "Holy Spirit" movement. In Spain those cultists were called the "Alumbrados." I treat this problem later in sections 4b and 4c of this chapter (pages 19 & 20). —J.W.S

to his heavenly Father **[278]**, dying in his Father's hands **[297]**, and instructing his disciples to baptize in the Name of the Father, and of the Son, and of the Holy Spirit **[307]**" (Egan, 1987, p. 81).

Ignatius focuses explicitly on the Father by asking the exercitant to conclude most of the meditations, contemplations, and colloquies with "the Lord's Prayer." The "Our Father" is the first prayer suggested for use in the Second and Third Methods of Prayer **[249, 258]**. Egan reiterates that "Ignatius expects the exercitant to experience transient consolations in which the creator both enters and leaves the soul **[322, 330]**," consolations that are free gifts that will provide strength in future trials. Moreover, Egan interprets that in these consolations the exercitant experiences God as *Father* (Egan, 1987, p. 81).

3. It is also a Christ-centered Mysticism.

It is clear from all of Ignatius' writings that the person and the personality of Jesus Christ had a profound influence on his conversion and on his entire life, including his mysticism. Ignatius regarded his recovery from seemingly mortal battle wounds as miraculous and due to Christ's personal intervention. The fact that he would suggest that the religious order that he was founding should bear the unprecedented title, "Company of Jesus" is testimony to the intensity of his dedication to Jesus Christ.

PMWYS
pp. 13–14

Ignatius was consumed by a "tremendous desire to labor in the Holy Land for the good of 'souls.' This desire for the Holy Land was a longing for Jesus, the concrete Jesus and no abstract idea.' [For example, on many occasions, as at Manresa or, on the ship to Jerusalem] "Ignatius received many visions and representations of Christ. He saw him, with mystical sight, as a white, undifferentiated body, or with white rays coming from above. He likewise saw how Christ was present in the Eucharist and he received special visions about Christ's humanity. These visions consoled Ignatius, pointed out a specific way of serving Christ, and confirmed him in this service." Ignatius often prayed to Mary, asking her to "Place Me With Your Son," a petition that was granted "at La Storta, where the Father placed Ignatius with Christ to serve them" (Egan, 1987, p. 87).

In Ignatian mysticism, mediators are important to the person seeking God. "The Ignatian mediator par excellence, of course, is Jesus Christ, the Son who intercedes with the Father, or the Son whose affairs the Father sets in order." In one of the several "types of visions that show still other aspects of his trinitarian and Jesus-centered mysticism, Ignatius grasped Jesus' divinity by way of his humanity. . . . The Ignatian Christ is always the Son of the Virgin Mary according to the flesh and the Son of the eternal Father" (Egan, 1987, pp. 89–93).

4. And, Ignatian Mysticism is of the Holy Spirit.

a. St. Paul's references to the Holy Spirit. St. Paul provides us with detailed assurance of divine, intercessory help: "The Spirit too helps us in our weakness, for we do not know how to pray as we ought; but the Spirit himself makes intercession for us with groanings that cannot be expressed in speech. He who searches hearts knows what the Spirit means, for the Spirit intercedes for the saints as God himself wills" (Rom. 8:26–27). This scriptural reassurance of the divinely guaranteed effectiveness of our prayers, in spite of distractions, desolation, or even despair should fill the retreatants with hope and courage.

b. Ignatius' references to the Holy Spirit. In the chapter entitled "A Trinitarian Mysticism", Egan devotes a section to "A Mysticism of the Holy Spirit." He points out that "references to the Holy Spirit abound in Ignatius' *Spiritual Diary,* attesting to the Holy Spirit's explicit presence in his mystical life. These references to the importance of the Holy Spirit are significant in the meditations that follow those of Day 3 in Week 3, and other places throughout the Exercises. Specifically I recommend a colloquy to the Holy Spirit for Day 4 of Week 3—a recommendation of which I believe Ignatius would now approve. But that would have been at least imprudent and probably even life-threatening had he done so in his own day when the atmosphere in the European Church was electric with charges and counter charges related to the distasteful excesses attributed to cult devotees of the Holy Spirit.

PMWYS *pp. 31–33*

c. Absence of references to the Holy Spirit by Ignatius in the Spiritual Exercises. Egan also notes that "the relative absence of references to the Holy Spirit in the *Spiritual Exercises* is striking. Yet one must remember how frequently Ignatius and his companions were jailed and interrogated for their teachings and their conspicuously different way of life. Church authorities suspected Ignatius and his companions of being *Alumbrados,* members of cultist religious movements that in their extreme forms claimed the direct and constant inspiration of the Holy Spirit. . . . It can be shown that Ignatius purposely paraphrased or dropped out some gospel texts or phrases used in the *Spiritual Exercises* to avoid mentioning the Holy Spirit, although the context of the unaltered gospel texts practically eliminates the possibility of an Alumbrados-like interpretation" (Egan, 1987, p. 83).

Yet Ignatius' other, more personal writings definitely link the Holy Spirit with his experiences of consolation, discernment, election, and confirmation. To do full justice to the meaning and the need for Spiritual Exercises therefore, one must understand them and make and direct them in the light of Ignatius' own Spirit mysticism. In fact, they depend more on an implicit experience of the Holy Spirit than the "safe" explicit references indicate" (Egan, 1987, pp. 83–84).

d. Gospel texts on the Holy Spirit. Those Gospel texts that Egan refers to in his section titled "A Mysticism of the Holy Spirit" are those in which the *Spiritual Exercises* refer to Elizabeth as being filled with the Holy Spirit **[263]**; when the Holy Spirit comes upon Jesus at his baptism **[273]**; when the risen Christ gives the apostles the Holy Spirit **[304]**; when Christ commands them to baptize in the name of the Father, Son, and Holy Spirit **[307]**; and when Christ tells them to await the coming of the Holy Spirit in Jerusalem **[307]**. Ignatius spoke clearly of the one Spirit which guides both the individual and the Church **[365]**, as well as later on in the safe context of the 'Rules for Thinking with the Church (Egan, 1987, p. 83). And even if Ignatius had not been so explicit in his devotion to the Holy Spirit, the Gospel of John would be authority enough to encourage intimacy with the Spirit. Also, compare the readings for Trinity Sunday, as well as the Gospel of Luke, "the Evangelist of the Holy Spirit" and the Evangelist of Prayer.

5. From God alone—"Consolation without previous cause."

A most important insight concerning the action of the Spirit in the exercitant relates to "consolation without previous cause." This experience is described by Ignatius as a property or capacity belonging "to God alone to give consolation to the soul without previous cause, for it belongs to the Creator to enter into the soul, to leave it, and to act upon it, drawing it wholly to the love of His Divine Majesty" **[330]**. Moreover, "there is no deception in it" **[336]**, because only God can give this type of consolation. For a further discussion of this type of consolation see Egan (1976, pp. 31–65; 140–41); and Toner (1982, pp. 216–22; 243–56; 291–313).

III. OVERVIEW AND DYNAMICS OF PHASE ONE: WEEKS 1 THROUGH 4

A. Preparing for Phase One prayer.

1. The discovery of the "Discernment" Method by Ignatius.

In preparation for Phase One prayer both exercitant and director should read briefly about the events that led Ignatius to discover his path in life. That great adventure started to take shape as he reflected on what gave him long lasting satisfaction and what left him with long term dissatisfaction—the basis for his most insightful "discernment of spirits" **[313–336]**. As director you should encourage an exercitant to reflect on those events or turning points in her life that have brought her to undertake this retreat. Emphasize the elements of satisfaction and dissatisfaction as also forming the basis for her "discernment of spirits."

PMWYS p. 13–14

2. Phase One—Intentional Differences from the Next Three Phases of the Ignatian Retreat.

For many directors and exercitants, the first phase may at first seem out of place because its pattern is so different from the phases that follow, dominated as the latter are by meditations on the life, death, and resurrection of Jesus. It is important that as Director you clearly see that Phase One is indeed part of the fabric of the four phases. One way to understand it is to realize that Phase One looks way back before the Incarnation and attempts to take the long view—God's view of the Universe, the Cosmos—God's prelude as our Father to the sending of his Son as the Redeemer of that Universe.

a. Goal of Phase One Exercises. The "creation oriented" exercises of Phase One are meant to stir an exercitant to see herself as a part of creation and, as such, to have and to realize a destiny whose purposes as a creature are consonant with those of the creator. In these mediations Ignatius wishes the exercitant to focus on the evidence of God's lavish and unconditional love all around and in all of creation and, because we are part of that creation, our true and deepest happiness and fulfillment is to be found in living that God-endowed role in harmony with God's purposes. The authentic living of that God-given role can be accomplished by freeing ourselves of fear and illusion, and living in faith, hope and love. This theme runs throughout Barry's *Now Choose Life*. It is not only one of the clearest statements of the spirit of Phase One but at the same time it also captures the excitement, adventure, and sense of solidarity with Christ pretty much as it must have enthralled Ignatius himself. By discovering the purposes of the creator, he saw that he himself as a product "of creation" could and should participate in a vital way in the grand adventure of the Universe. He later concretizes that adventure by joining forces with Jesus, the Incarnate God, whom we are privileged to know both in the pages of the Gospels, and in our own hearts through contemplation.

b. How Phase One differs from the other three. The Second, Third, and Fourth Phases of the *Exercises* have a clearly developed and appealing Christological pattern since they are focused on events from the life, passion, death, resurrection, and post-resurrection appearances of Jesus. At first glance the Christology of Phase One is not as conspicuous, but it is equally important, and thus deserves explicit attention on the part of the director. Excellent treatments are also found in Egan (1987, pp. 98–100); and in Rahner, (1968, pp. 59–93; 1994, pp. 192–97). The meditations of the first four weeks of Phase One are meant to situate the exercitant cosmically with respect to creation and to God, the Creator. Here Ignatius is concerned with the superabundant love for mankind manifested in creation, and mankind's proper response to the recognizable fact that as part of that creation there are corresponding God-given responsibilities and God-given opportunities (Weeks 1 and 2). Although he has not been cited widely in studies on the Spiritual Exercises, Teilhard de Chardin's writings illuminate in a contemporary idiom and in a most energizing way the Ignatian spirituality of the Exercises. Teilhard's last major essay, *The Heart of Matter,* was written in 1950. It is replete with ideas of the theme of God's creation of the Universe, and of mankind's role in helping to bring the Kingdom of God to completion. (1976, 1979). Meditations drawn from several of Teilhard's writings are cited throughout PMWYS and are intended to help to constructively illuminate significant Ignatian themes.

B. *Dynamics of the "Phase One Experience"—from Consolation to Desolation*

PMWYS pp. 21, 25, 39

As the exercitant immerses herself in the retreat she may commonly feel much consoled after having been praying in praise and thanksgiving in the spirit of the recommended psalms for Weeks 1, 2, and 4. Then experiences of desolation, or a sense of alienation or spiritual impotence often surface. It is at this time that the director needs to remind the exercitant of the practical need for discernment of spirits. At this point the exercitant may even feel completely unworthy of God, often doubting the earlier good experiences.

DYNAMICS OF "PHASE ONE EXPERIENCE"

The exercitant will benefit from reading a short summary of what Barry explained in a 1973 study. He points out that consolation early in the retreat may have resulted from the exercitant praying from strength, rather than from weakness. Not that there is anything wrong with so doing at that time. Yet typically as one gets into the retreat, one can begin to be so overwhelmed by an increased sensitivity to one's own weaknesses that desolation is experienced *now,* and the feeling of being needy is *now*—a distasteful and even frightening emotional state. Such an experience of alienation is related to each one's own history of sin and failures. This innermost experience, if it is to be salutary, must be discerned for what it is—a recognition of both that early strength, and an honest facing up to one's weakness and sinfulness. At the same time, the unconditional love of Jesus for us *now* is for each *as* an individual. Once we face squarely the fact of self as sinner and that our strength is only in the saving strength of Jesus' grace, that sense of alienation, of fear, and of abandonment will all drain away. Thus, by working through this process we will have entered upon a fruitful pattern of discernment. Chapter 4, "Repent and Believe the Good News" is an insightful sequel to this discussion in *Now Choose Life* (Barry, 1990, pp. 30–43).

The focus and goal of the Exercises of Phase One is clearly and simply said in the author's words: "Imagining Christ our Lord present and placed on the Cross. . . . let me make a Colloquy. . . ." **[53]**. "The same thing may well happen to the sinner as happened to Ignatius at Manresa when he was starting his anguished contemplations of sin and the mystically inspired woman uttered those words. . . . 'O may it please my Lord Jesus Christ to appear to you one day!' And this is precisely how the crucified Christ 'appears' to the sinner during his meditations of the first" Phase—"with a sublime suddenness, as the central point of the whole of salvation history, into which even the exercitant's own personal sinfulness appears to become completely subsumed. . . . It is significant . . . that Ignatius should have included in his *Exercises* that ancient prayer which he loved so much—the Anima Christi." As a great Ignatian scholar has pointed out: "This was not just a touching example of his own personal devotion; it was the deliberate announcement of a theme which runs through all that follows." (Rahner, 1968, pp. 59–60).

PMWYS *p. 17*

1. Awareness Meditation, a Buddhist-Christian method of prayer—Key to interior silence, focusing, and discernment: Weeks 1 & 2.

Because I regard Awareness Meditation as fundamental for meditation practice, I introduced it at the beginning of the retreat. Week 1 of Phase One serves basically as an introduction to the good kind of awareness meditation that I regard as essential to finding God in all things. Many who are drawn to prayer lose interest after a time because prayer time is full of "distractions." Basically, awareness meditation is a way of deliberately quieting the mind and emotions so that one may not only focus prayerfully and reverently during formal meditation but also have a way to "let go" of all other preoccupying thoughts. It allows one to be aware of and to center on the "one thing necessary" and to sit at the feet of Jesus, like Mary, or to walk like the disciples on the way to Emmaus. This is required to cultivate the spirit of the contemplative in action and to find God in all of what is done to one and in all of what one does.

In fact, I believe that Ignatius presupposed the basic principles underlying awareness meditation, chief among which is summed up in a phrase attributed to him, "*Age quod agis*—Do what you are doing." I interpret that aphorism to mean: focus on, be immersed in, develop an increasing sensitivity to, and give your undivided attention in a dynamically relaxed fashion to whatever you are conscious of and alive to in all your sensibility *and* totally. Eastern meditation practice is preoccupied with self awareness, even as Ignatius is. For this reason it seems to me that special attention must be given to the daily practice of awareness. As indicated there, the most important meditation of the day in the view of Ignatius is the very simple but often underestimated Awareness Examen.

PMWYS
pp. 10–12, 39

Awareness meditations commonly are mistrusted or passed over lightly because in and of themselves they seem not to be "religious" or to have religious content. As presented by deMello in *Sadhana: A Way to God*, such exercises not only help the exercitant to quiet down and focus preliminary to formal prayer, but also to attain the resulting stillness which is a way of letting go of nagging fears and burdens. To make the experience Christological, one has only to recall Jesus' promise, "Come to me, all you who are weary and heavily burdened and I will refresh you." Retreatants and college seniors in my seminar on geology and spirituality tell me how important these awareness meditations are in helping to free them of career-related fears and the pressures that are part of every family's life.

2. *Supreme Importance of the Principle and Foundation.*

The director should be aware that most students of the Spiritual Exercises generally consider the Principle and Foundation as articulated by Ignatius to be the basis on which all the retreat experience is grounded, and thus they place it before the exercises of Phase One. While acknowledging its supreme importance, however, I believe that some fundamental preparations for such considerations and prayer are required. Thus I place the Principle and Foundation in Week 2 with Awareness Meditation exercises in both Weeks 1 and 2 so that the exercitant may build up this experiential Foundation on a solid substrate of centered awareness.

3. *Insights into the Principle and Foundation of Ignatian spirituality: Week 2.*

In the retreat as developed here, Week 2, begins with what Ignatius calls the Principle and Foundation **[23]**. It is a central action of the *Exercises,* and, as Egan says: "a meditation designed to impart to the exercitant a vivid sense of life's meaning, goal, and the means to obtain this goal. . . . From the outset, therefore, Ignatius strives to awaken exercitants to Christian wisdom, that is, to a holistic, total vision wherein everything is seen in its proper place [in relation to everything else].

The writings of St. Paul provided Teilhard de Chardin with just such a cosmic perspective on life's meaning and goal and on the means of attaining that goal "to bring all things in the heavens and on earth into one under Christ's headship" (Eph. 1: 9–10, 22–23). It seems clear that Paul places the Body of Christ theme squarely in a cosmic framework and at the same time presents the relationship between Christ and the cosmos as an extension of the physical and sacramental relationship between Christ and the members of the Church. Not only is Christ Lord of the Universe, he is also its 'Head' (1 Cor. 1:15–20). These Pauline concepts, reaffirmed sixteen centuries later by Ignatius in "The Principle and Foundation," are reiterated anew, in Teilhard's dynamic and evolutive terms that convey strongly motivational meaning to the twentieth-century inhabitants of the same cosmos.

a. Finding God in All Things. Continuing with Egan: "Moreover, we should see all creatures as 'bathed in the blood of Christ'. . . . In short, the Ignatian formula, 'finding God in all things,' can mean finding the trinitarian Christ in all things, or even finding all things in the trinitarian Christ. The Ignatian person must desire only Christ and him crucified, because Jesus Christ is the beginning, middle, and end of all good. 'All our wickedness,' according to Ignatius, 'shall be entirely consumed, when our souls shall be completely penetrated and possessed by Him and our wills . . .transformed into His will. . .'" (Egan, 1987, p. 96). In essence, the implementation of the Principle and Foundation which establishes our indifference to all created things "must be seen in the light of a passionate love and service of Jesus Christ, the Creator and Lord of all . . . 'Indifference to all created things' is actually an Ignatian mysticism of joy in the world because it was created in, through, and for Christ." (Egan, p. 98). Other annotations of the Exercises that adumbrate aspects of the Principle and Foundation are found in **[16, 65, 98, 109, 130, 196, 223–24, and 234–36]**. (See, for context, Egan, pp. 96–98.)

b. The Principle and Foundation—a compendium of the Exercises. The brevity with which Ignatius states the Principle and Foundation has often been and still sometimes is misinterpreted as a rigid, cut and dried, intellectual formula for achieving personal sanctity **[23]**. However, it must not be regarded merely as a philosophical proposition to be pondered intellectually but as a conscientious summing up of the spiritual exercising needed before deliberately selecting one's state of life. It can only be properly appreciated in the light of the contemplations of the King and of the two Flags (Standards) and to the procedure of the Election **[169, 175–188]**. Hence the Foundation is simply a highly compressed theological compendium of the whole of the *Exercises*, and it can only be understood in terms of the *vocatio regis*, 'the call of the King.'" (Rahner, 1968, p. 62).

In these meditations Ignatius is reacting to the discovery of the excess of love manifest in God's act of creating the cosmos of which mankind is a part. However, we created humans are prone to frequently react to our Creator's creating actions with fear instead of with friendship and love. The statement of the Principle and Foundation is calculated to help us overcome that and establish a right attitude toward the things of the world, a hunger for their evolving goodness as integral to creation, whether past, present, or future. This statement calls it "the longing for those things which help *more* toward the end for which we have been created" (Rahner, 1968, p. 61). Basically this means that the exercitant's goal in life, the measure of his success, will be tied to efforts to live in harmony with his role as part of God's creation. "In this rather abstract statement [on the Principle and Foundation], Ignatius spells out the implications of experiencing that we are all created with the desire for union with God and that nothing but such union will satisfy us" (Barry, 1991, p. 462).

c. Fear and the Principle and Foundation—Week 2. In the Principle and Foundation (Week 2 of Phase One), Ignatius was well aware however, of the obstacles to be hurdled as we undertake a lifelong journey towards an ultimate intimacy with Jesus that is consistent with the way that we human beings are able to move from the relationship of "stranger" or "quasi-stranger" to friend and, ultimately, to lover. As humans, that relational growth usually cannot happen instantly or over night. For the most part too, our relationship to God must grow and mature slowly. Rich insights into the human and personal meaning of the Principle and Foundation also emerge in Barry's article on "Founding A Relationship with God" (*America*, 1991, p. 458).

DYNAMICS OF "PHASE ONE EXPERIENCE"

***PMWYS** pp. 24–30*

Barry first cites *Death of a Naturalist,* a poem by Seamus Heaney who uses the metaphor of scaffolding to say something profound about the build-up of fear and the barrier that it may set against a relationship with a loved one. We are also reminded how we can fan the fire of our friendship with and love for Christ by the story of the fox who asked Saint-Exupéry's Little Prince to become his friend—actions that led to a sound relationship and eventually to intimacy. In sum, Barry says "Even though every human being is constantly being drawn by divine love toward union with God, we all have conflicting desires as well. Fear gets in the way of our desire to become more intimate with God" (*America,* 1991, p.462). As the director, you should not only read this article but you should also have the exercitants do so, because it captures in a gripping way the ambivalence that we all sometimes experience—of fear or at least of discomfort from the mixed prospect of intimacy and possible rejection.

d. Pauline texts on God, the Creator's love for us. Aspects of the Principle and Foundation have been also revealed to us by Paul in Ephesians 3:9 where he reminds us that God is "the Creator of all" and that we exist as such, because God wished us into being and keeps us so. Earlier, the Apostle to the Gentiles had made it clear that the Gentiles, including ourselves, are the beneficiaries of the "unfathomable riches of Christ" and that now we have the opportunity to be enlightened "on the mysterious design which for ages was hidden in God, the Creator of all." (Eph 1 & 2). It is abundantly clear from revelation then that God is completely in love with us and finds us, his creation, utterly attractive. The difficulty is that most of us find that nearly impossible to believe—but we must try to overcome our secret conflicting fears of a powerful God, one who is all too ready to scold us and to punish us. If unbelief wins, our attraction to God deep within our very being may be stunted, or it may go unrecognized or even be paralyzed by fear of God. To overcome this we need to experience God as attractive; we need to give God an opportunity to show us that he is in fact the central object of our love and desire. Paul recognized this and from prison generated hope by assuring his followers: "In Christ and through faith in him we can speak freely to God, drawing near him with confidence" (Eph. 3:12).

e. Ignatian meaning of "being indifferent to all created things." Frederick Buechner says in his autobiography, *Sacred Journey*, that "From such experiences" [of exquisite joy] "Ignatius came to see that the universe is a place where God is continually drawing each and every one of us into the community life of the Trinity. It is as though the three Persons in God, the perfect community of Father, Son and Holy Spirit, say to one another 'Our community life is so rich and satisfying. Why don't we create a universe where we can invite other persons into our community life?'

Ignatius invites us to take seriously these foundational experiences of God creating us out of love and for a loving community. For such a pearl of great value we would want nothing to get in the way, which is what Ignatius meant by the notion of being indifferent to all created things. Not that we do not care for things, but that we do not want to be so attached to any of them that we would miss the pearl of great price, which is to be in tune with God's creative purpose in creating the universe and each one of us" (Barry, 1991, p. 462)

So, like that sensitive and perceptive Presbyterian minister, we must realize sometime on our journey that once we experience a desire for a more intimate relationship with God we need to nurture it by making time for God to draw us closer. So think of the fox as you pray and if you are fearful, tell God of your fear honestly. That is the real meaning of the Principle and Foundation.

4. Insights into the essence of Week 3: Self-inflicted wounds and Spirit-inspired healing—Sin and the Great Struggle.

Returning to Egan, we see that he also regards Phase One as really beginning "after the Principle and Foundation exercise. It focuses upon the cosmic and historical unity of the mystery of evil. The exercitant must consider the cosmic origin of sin in the fall of the angels **[50]**, the beginnings of sin in human history through the fall of Adam and Eve **[51]**" as portrayed in the Genesis narrative, 'the particular sin of any person who went to hell because of one mortal sin' **[52]**, the history of one's personal sins **[55–61]**, and finally sin's ultimate consequence: hell **[65–71]**" (Barry, 1987, p. 98). These meditations are not merely fanciful pastimes. They embody the Christology of sin that helps to clarify in stark terms "what is meant by the statement that the Messiah came in order to destroy the works of the devil" (Rahner, 1968, p. 99). It should be recognized that the language in these annotations and some of the historical and theological perspectives on them have undergone some readjustments in recent decades. Nevertheless, Ignatius' vision of the cosmic and historical pervasiveness of sin and the cosmic and personal struggle in which Christ and we are engaged is fundamental. The consoling idea is that although sinfulness and sin are pervasive, they are more than matched by God's mercy and forgiveness.

DYNAMICS OF "PHASE ONE EXPERIENCE"

All the Phase One contemplations on sin end at Calvary with Jesus the crucified. There the exercitant, faced with the revelation of self as a redeemed sinner, reflects in personal terms on the questions: "what have I done for Christ, what am I doing for Christ, what ought I do for Christ?" **[53]**. And these questions are contemplated by the exercitant with great gratitude and even amazement at God's mercy **[60]**. Thus by comprehending sin and salvation in relation to Jesus Christ and after listening to Christ's call in the Kingdom meditations **[91–100]**, Phase One is linked to the Incarnation, a pivotal exercise in Phase Two **[101–109]**. Ultimately the exercitant responds to the three questions asked at Calvary—either by making an election or by making certain choices and a commitment to living in the third degree of humility **[167]**.

5. Day 1 Meditation illustrates the Need for the Discernment of Spirits.

The meditation as presented by Ignatius for Day 1 of Week 3, the story of David and Bathsheba, does not deal explicitly with the discernment of spirits. However, that biblical story of sin, repentance, and conversion (2 Samuel 11:1–12:15) illustrates dramatically the discernment "rules" or guidelines that Ignatius considered especially suitable for the First Phase **[313–336]**. As retreat director you have an opportunity here to point out that these rules are central to the dynamic of the Ignatian Exercises since they outline the strategy of the good and evil spirits insofar as the process of discernment involves spiritual consolation **[316 & 323–27]** and spiritual desolation **[317–22]**. Ignatius begins these guidelines as follows:

PMWYS pp. 31–32

[313] **RULES**

FOR PERCEIVING AND KNOWING IN SOME MANNER

THE DIFFERENT MOVEMENTS WHICH ARE CAUSED IN THE SOUL

THE GOOD, TO RECEIVE THEM AND THE BAD TO REJECT THEM. AND THEY ARE MORE PROPER FOR THE FIRST WEEK.

[314] ***FIRST RULE. The First Rule: In the persons who go from mortal sin to mortal sin, the enemy is commonly used to propose to them apparent pleasures, making them imagine sensual delights and pleasures in order to hold them more and make them grow in their vices and sins. In these persons the good spirit uses the opposite method, pricking them and biting their consciences through the process of reason.***

The story of David and Bathsheba is used to illustrate the application of Ignatius' points contained in his "rules" for discernment of spirits (Barry, 1990, pp. 44–55). Not only did David commit adultery, but he committed further crimes, including the murder not only of Uriah, Bathsheba's soldier husband, but also of other soldiers who unwittingly were party to the coverup. One sin led to another, as Samuel reports, quoting David's reassurance to the commanding officer who carried out his deadly order: "Don't let this upset you, the sword devours one as well as another" (2 Sam 11: 24–25). Up to this point David gave no hint of remorse, being totally caught up in his illusions. But God opened David's eyes to the truth of his sinful state through Nathan, the prophet, resulting in David's anguished cry of repentance, "I have sinned against the Lord."

In *Now Choose Life: Conversion as the Way to Life*, there is a nuanced treatment of Ignatius' "Rules" that illustrates anecdotally how realistic and modern Ignatius was as an observer of the human and divine condition. Barry summarizes "conversion as a gift of God drawing us progressively away from illusion into the reality of the created universe and of God." Another engaging contemporary treatment of the strategy of the evil spirit is made by C. S. Lewis in *The Screwtape Letters*. And a broad-ranging discussion of various aspects of discernment can be found in

Weeds Among the Wheat—Discernment: Where Prayer and Action Meet by Thomas H. Green, S.J.

DYNAMICS OF "PHASE ONE EXPERIENCE"

The spirit in which Jesus deals with sinners is well illustrated in a number of passages in Luke, the evangelist called by Dante the "scribe of Christ's gentleness" because of his emphasis on Jesus' mercy to sinners and outcasts. "Some of the most memorable Gospel stories of divine mercy are found only in Luke (the widow of Naim, the prodigal son, and Zacchaeus)." Some of Luke's prominent themes are salvation for all, mercy and forgiveness, and the joy of salvation. (See Kodell, in CBC, pp. 936–38 for specific texts).

6. Quadruple Colloquy explicitly includes the Holy Spirit.

As a retreat director you should be aware that in the *Spiritual Exercises* Ignatius commonly urges the exercitant to engage in a Triple Colloquy—that is, with God the Father, with Jesus, his Son, and with Mary, the Mother of Jesus. In the third edition of *Place Me With Your Son*, you will note that the exercitant is urged to engage in a Quadruple Colloquy, including one to the Holy Spirit. You may be asked about the reason for this departure from what is perceived to be the Ignatian tradition.

PMWYS *p. 33 & throughout*

The reason for introducing the Quadruple Colloquy is as follows: "Most commentators [on the *Spiritual Exercises* of Ignatius] agree that Ignatius' mysticism is first and foremost trinitarian" (Egan, 1987, pp. 66–85) Indeed, in Chapter 3, "A Trinitarian Mysticism," Harvey Egan devotes a section to "A Mysticism of the Holy Spirit." He points out that "references to the Holy Spirit abound in Ignatius' *Spiritual Diary*, attesting to the Holy Spirit's explicit presence in his mystical life." However, in the Autograph there is no explicit mention of a Colloquy with the Holy Spirit. Nevertheless, the more personal writings of Ignatius that survive definitely link the Holy Spirit with his experiences of consolation, discernment, election, and confirmation. (See also Section B, 1 & herein.)

a. Ignatius' Own Spirit Mysticism. "To do full justice to the Spiritual Exercises, therefore, one must understand them and give them in the light of Ignatius' own Spirit mysticism" (Egan, 1987, pp. 83–84). Since the storm clouds of the Spanish Inquisition, and its slightly more sophisticated counterpart, Anti-Modernism, have both blown over, it seems reasonable that if Ignatius were writing and editing the *Spiritual Exercises* today, he would include a colloquy to the Holy Spirit. In the Autograph text of *The Spiritual Exercises,* Ignatius refers to Gospel texts that "present Elizabeth as being filled with the Holy Spirit **[263]**; the Holy Spirit comes upon Jesus at his baptism **[273]**; the risen Christ gives the apostles the Holy Spirit **[304]**; he commands them to baptize in the name of the Father, Son, and Holy Spirit **[307]**; and he tells them to await the coming of the Holy Spirit in Jerusalem **[312]**. Ignatius spoke of the one Spirit which guides both the individual and the Church **[365]**, but only in the safe context of the 'Rules for Thinking with the Church'" (Egan, 1987, p.83).

b. Luke—"Evangelist of the Holy Spirit." This is an appropriate place to note that Luke is sometimes referred to as "the Evangelist of the Holy Spirit" and the "Evangelist of Prayer." For specific citations concerning the Holy Spirit see Kodell (CBC, 1989, p. 938) who points out that the Father's guidance of Jesus and the fledgling church highlights the role of the Holy Spirit. And even if Luke had not emphasized the Holy Spirit, John's Gospel would be authority enough to encourage intimacy with the Spirit. Consult the readings for Trinity Sunday also.

Thus in the light of the clear evidence that the Exercises are permeated with trinitarian mysticism, and that both Ignatius' writings and the four gospels are explicitly Spirit oriented, I have modified the "third exercise" **[62]** and have introduced the Quadruple or Four-fold Colloquy. I suggest that each exercitant engage in it during the meditation on Day 4 of Week 3 and in colloquies that follow.

7. Dynamics of Week 4: A sinner loved by God.

Before the transition week devoted to the *"The Call and the Coming of the Eternal King,"* the final week of meditations in Phase One focuses, as week 4, on the exercitant asking for the gift of experiencing himself as a loved sinner. However, that recognition has already come to a kind of halt, not in self-centered complacency but in order to seek a purification and "a growing desire for conversion, insight into the tactics of God's enemy and a renewed enthusiasm to follow Jesus." Once you have that enthusiasm, or even a desire for it, you may be ready to make the transition to Phase Two.

PMWYS
p. 38

IV. TRANSITION FROM PHASE ONE TO PHASE TWO

A. Balancing the Liturgical Year Readings and the Ignatian Retreat Meditations

When the retreat's subject matter is not parallel with that of the liturgical year, as happens when a retreat begins at the end of November, how should the exercitants proceed? In general I find it useful to follow the *Spiritual Exercises* as St. Ignatius designed them, since they have their own logic and dynamic. Even so, the liturgical year may only be about a week or two ahead of the retreat stages. For example, the meditations of Week 4 on *"A Sinner Loved by God"* which end Phase One and the considerations on *The Call and Coming of the Eternal King* of Week 5 which are transitional between Phase One and Phase Two. may fall around Christmas. Then in January the meditations of Week 6 deal with *The Incarnation and Birth of Jesus* and those of Week 7 focus on *The "Showing Forth" of the Newborn King.*

PMWYS pp. 46–48

I suggest that as director you encourage exercitants to place prime emphasis on the basic progress of the retreat's subject matter, but at the same time to weave aspects of the incarnation and the birth of Jesus into the meditations, because they are suitable to the liturgical celebrations, especially in Christmas time. For example, while contemplating the meditations of Week 4, they could center, in part, on the concept that many of the injustices prevalent in today's world are due to ignorance of, or rejection of, the Gospel values. One might also reflect on some of the ways in which Jesus, Mary and Joseph, in the events leading up to the birth of Jesus and later in their flight into Egypt, experienced the effects of the sins of others in one way or another.

In the layer by layer build-up of the dynamics of the complete *Spiritual Exercises*, Ignatius proposes to each exercitant a salutary Advent experience of one's own sinfulness. As First Phase meditations, these experiential reflections help prepare us for the actualization of the presence of Jesus in our daily lives in a more complete and fulfilling way than ever before. Phase Two begins with Week 6, and consists of formal meditations on the Incarnation and Birth of Jesus. However, since Christmas and the liturgical remembrance of Jesus birth may well be upon you before the completion of the four weeks of Phase One, I urge you to let the Spirit's gentle movements determine the interplay of meditation topics that will best inspire the praying of your exercitants' prayer over that period.

B. *Dynamics of Week 5: Creation, a personal call to high adventure—The Call and the Coming of the Eternal King.*

1. *"About the King" or the Imitation of Christ*

PMWYS
p. 46

Ignatius uses the term "About the King" and presents this exercise as a consideration calculated to lead to contemplation. For many of us today, the reference to the Call of the King or meditations on a royal kingdom have little intellectual or emotional appeal **[91–98]**. However, we, all of us as citizens of whatever polity, are responsive to a true Leader who is altruistic, unselfish, and who will fight for his people even if it costs his life. "This exercise is concerned mainly with the challenging call by the risen Jesus to follow him." Ignatius' consideration of a royal leader, although somewhat trapped in another time, is a most appropriate analogy that all can respond to with great generosity. As director, you will probably know your exercitants well enough to help them visualize the kind of a good and great Leader who can really challenge them to a life of high adventure and whom they can follow with complete generosity.

Indeed, as Ignatius, with his acute sensitivity to Holy Scripture, did after his Manresa experience, we can seize the opportunity to grasp the essence of the mysteries of salvation as a coherent whole. This is well explained by the author of *Ignatius the Theologian* who points out that "the somewhat amorphous ideas that Ignatius had noted down from the *Life of Christ* had now been developed into the *Mystery of the life of Christ*" (Rahner, 1968, p. 97).

"The ideal of the King and the Two Standards was not unknown before, but as a result of this constructive transformation it took on a completely new meaning: henceforth Christ the eternal King was for Ignatius to be a living King actively at work here and now in this world, who has not completely fulfilled the mission given him by his Father to bring the whole world under his rule, and who, therefore, is here and now seeking noble and generous companions and friends who desire to prove their loyalty in battle" (Rahner, 1953, p. 56, n.63).

The cosmic notion of Christ as king of the Universe is a dominant theme in the writings of Teilhard de Chardin. His approach basically takes three passages from St. Paul's letters (Eph. 1: 9–10, 22–23; Col. 1:15–20; and Ro. 8:19–23) two of which I commented on earlier in this manual in the discussion of the Principle and Foundation. Teilhard illuminates and extends

Ignatius' picture of Christ as King by interpreting in light of modern science Paul's texts as having an evolutionary and cosmic significance. In the letter to the faithful at Ephesus, Paul presents Christ as supreme over all cosmic forces: "God has given us the wisdom to understand fully the mystery, the plan he was pleased to decree in Christ, to be carried out in the fullness of time: namely to bring all things in the heavens and on earth into one under Christ's headship . . . He has put all things under Christ's feet and has made him, thus exalted, head of the church, which is his body: the fullness of him who fills the universe in all its parts." (Eph. 1:9–10)

Teilhard in a 1930 lecture describes Christ as the one "in whom all has been created and he in whom the whole world finds its stability, with all its height and depth, its grandeur and greatness, with all that is material and all that is spiritual" (cited by Mooney, 1964, p. 100). Christ is presented preeminently as the Head or King of creation by Paul (Col. 1:15–20): "He is the image of the invisible God, the first-born of all creatures. In him everything in heaven and on earth was created, things visible and invisible . . . all were created through him, and for him. He is before all else that is. In him everything continues in being. It is he who is head of the body, the church; he who is the beginning, the first-born of the dead, so that primacy may be his in everything. It pleased God to make absolute fullness reside in him, and by means of him, to reconcile everything in his person, both on earth and in the heavens, making peace through the blood of his cross."

Paul insists that it is the whole of creation, including mankind which is the object of redemption (Ro. 8:19–23). Moreover, because Jesus came among us as God incarnate and was buried in the earth and rose again, it is precisely through the bodies of humans that redemption extends to the rest of creation (Mooney, 1964, pp. 89–103; Rahner 1994, pp. 192–97).

It is important for you as retreat director to guide the exercitant to share what is somewhat elusive but characteristic of Ignatius—"his acute sense of the 'sacramental' structure of the life of Christ. The whole earthly existence of the Word was one long parable of things invisible, and thus the exercitant is made to contemplate the visible life of God—in the 'synagogues, towns and villages where Christ our Lord went about preaching **[91]**, in order that he may 'smell and taste the infinite fragrance and sweetness of the divinity' **[124]**." This is the kind of awareness and conscious perception that Ignatius urges **[104]** when he tells each of us "to ask for interior knowledge of the Lord who became man for me, so that I may love him more and follow him" (Rahner, 1968, p. 98).

"The whole life of Christ and his death was one continuous battle against Satan—it was *the* contest with the adversary from the beginning. Thus for Ignatius the life of Christ was more than just an edifying example . . . it was the fundamental theological principle behind Christian spiritual life, which is ultimately nothing more nor less than the conforming of one's whole being through grace with the crucified and risen Lord of glory" (Rahner, 1968, p. 99).

2. *The Call of Christ to Each One of Us.*

Ignatius "concretizes the mercy of God in the exercise entitled "Christ the King and His Call" **[91–98]**. . . . He not only identifies himself as our personal savior but invites each man, woman, and child to be involved with him in working **[93]** for the salvation of fellow men and women and their world. The victory [95-glory] has been won in Christ, though it is still in process in us and in our world. . . . Ignatius proposes that we consider the response which a very generous person would make to Jesus, but he very carefully does not demand that we make the same response **[97–98]**. In fact, no colloquy is outlined, though a grace has been sought in terms of hearing and responding to the Call of Christ **[91]**.

PMWYS *pp. 46–47*

3. *The "Foundation of the Second Phase."*

Commentators commonly describe "The Call of Christ" as the "Foundation of the Second Phase." Ignatius provides guidance for this transition week, indicating that this exercise should be experienced twice **[99]**, The common, more leisurely practice of this as a repose or break period between the Phases draws its inspiration from the instruction by Ignatius to drop from the seven exercises a week in Phase One to only two formal periods of prayer before Phase Two. As director, you need to convey to the exercitant that most of this week-long period is different from both the preceding activity and that which is to follow. The "day" referred to in **[99]** for this transition period refers to the 30-day secluded retreat and thus, should be about a week long in this Nineteenth Annotation retreat. This break in the intensive, formal prayer provides an opportunity to go back in informal prayer and in one's journal to reflect on what has been consoling and what has been difficult or has given rise to blockages. "The Call of Christ is meant to rouse in the exercitant not only a generous response of gratitude but the commitment to the person of Jesus and to his work. The Kingdom exercise, then acts as a bridge between the gratitude for the mercy of God seen in

Christ in the First Phase and the study of his person and his work in the succeeding Phases. The Kingdom exercise at the same time is an encounter with Jesus as he is now—our risen Savior—who continues to invite each one of us to be his apostle for our own time and place."

DYNAMICS OF WEEK 5

PMWYS pp. 47–48

4. Modern difficulties with the concept of "King".

The retreat director should be sensitive to the fact that for some, the image of King may be either uninspiring or, especially for many women, may even conjure up thoughts and emotional overtones of regal domination by men. It is commonly the case, even on the part of dedicated women who not only project a strong personality but who are indeed strong, to be somewhat compulsively subordinate to husbands and children during much of their lives. Problems arise if and when that kind of dedication, enthusiastically entered into early on by many women, later generates a sense of having been exploited or otherwise disaffected, and results in the feeling that large elements of their lives may have been relatively unfulfilled in the process. Such persons may respond to God, not as King and Master but as Liberator or Friend who invites and "empowers one to become who I am supposed to be."

The above statements, when they arise and are articulated in the group sharing, may be subject to misunderstanding. Sometimes individuals who make them may be thought to be selfish and to have been unduly affected by "women's liberation." It is important here to call to mind Annotation **[22]** in which Ignatius wisely provides a guideline that the director and the exercitant are always to put a favorable interpretation on each other's statements so as to avoid misinterpretation and so that a correct understanding may develop. Not uncommonly a person in such a situation will recognize that it is possible to be liberated from the compulsion that produces what amounts to self-destructive behavior, and may develop a healthy and constructive form of self development. Not uncommonly, also, such liberation has the effect of helping to liberate the spouse and children from a correlative and deleterious form of self-destructive behavior as well.

PMWYS p. 4, § 5

One of the most common fruits of the retreat is recognizing God as Liberator and Patient Friend. Both of these concepts or images commonly go together and combine to free one from the compulsions that everyone seems to have. One that I can personally admit to in public is a compulsion to stick with a rigid self-imposed schedule and to be fairly inflexible with the resulting self-inflicted deadlines. While this is not terminally debilitating, it tends to destroy flexibility and spontaneity in dealing with the questions and problems of others. I notice, for example, that when I "let go" of my schedule in favor of a satisfying unscheduled discussion of a mutually interesting scientific or spirituality question, both of us go away enriched and happier. Perhaps one can put this "letting go so as to attend to the greater good" into theological terms, if it is seen that the element involved is what Rahner calls "the mysticism of everyday life." In that process of letting go of compulsions, am I not grasped by God whose heart softens and enlarges my own so that it can become more like the generous heart that the Creator meant it to be?

5. "Letting Go" in order to have the Pearl of Great Price.

The previously considered "letting go" may well lead the exercitant to more easily reflect on the value of patience in developing a solid spirituality. Commonly due to greed, impatience is a form of anger, a kind of "not-letting-go" with a vengeance—destructive certainly to one's peace of mind if not also to civil, kind relationships with others. It has been said, and I believe it, that impatience is the greatest obstacle to a constructive, and intimate relationship with God. No intimate relationship can long survive chronic impatience. An attitude of patience, especially in adversity, is a form of letting go of antagonistic control and a key to true peace of mind, which is in turn indispensable to fruitful meditation and contemplation, and certainly required to "leave behind all things in order to follow Christ." A recommended book on feminist theology that takes such behavior into account is *Transforming Grace* by Ann Carr.

C. Preparation for Phase Two Prayer that is devoted to Contemplation of the Life of Christ.

1. Praying out of one's strength.

Exercitants who have enjoyed a deep Phase One experience generally come to the contemplation of the life of Christ with enthusiasm and gratitude. In fact, the contemplation of Jesus may be not only enjoyable but easy. However, the director should be aware that an exercitant, while rejoicing in consolation, may also be concentrating "on Jesus kindness' and sympathy, his care for the sick and suffering" and . . . "may not advert to or take seriously, for example, the opposition Jesus encounters, even though this is explicitly presented. If [this is] so, remind the exercitant that this probably means that you are praying out of your strength . . ." (Barry, 1973, pp. 100–101).

CONTEMPLATIVE PRAYER OF PHASE TWO

2. *Praying out of one's weakness or after setbacks.*

When the novelty wears off, prayer is less enthralling, boredom sets in and the words repeat, and prayer is obviously not a prayer out of one's strength. "If the foregoing happens you will have to attend more carefully to elements in the life of Christ and in your prayer that will be more difficult. Then the exercitant may be praying out of weakness or even out of desolation." In fact, the doldrum period may presage another conversion experience similar to that described for Phase One, and may even be a kind of hidden resistance to entering this experience as he/she is becoming aware of the "cost of discipleship" and perhaps resisting without even becoming aware of it (Barry, 1973, pp. 100–101).

PMWYS *pp. 53*

D. The contemplative prayer of Phase Two.

1. *Centering on the Cross.*

Basically the Cross on which we "center" casts its shadow across the landscape of all the Retreat and especially in Phase Two. This is because "these meditations are a preparation for the Election, where the exercitant has to order his life in accordance with the lessons they teach him. This election, too, is at times subject to the basic antithesis of *labor* and *gloria* **[93 & 95]**; in biblical terms it expresses an insight into . . . misunderstanding of Messiahship: that it was necessary that Christ should suffer these things and so enter into his glory (Lk 24: 25–6; 24: 44–6; 1 Pt 1: 10–12)" (See Rahner, 1968, p.100).

Moreover, "it is important always to bear in mind the ultimate aim of the Spiritual Exercises when considering the development of these contemplations: Ignatius intended the life of Christ to be seen, within the context of salvation, as the great exemplar of a choice, culminating in the cross. (Heb. 12: 2)" (See Rahner, 1968, p. 101).

2. *Listening to the Spirit singlemindedly and prudently in order to understand interior movements.*

Note that Ignatius sets down a number of additional guidelines that are focused on deepening the contemplations of Phase Two so as to maximize their impact. As director of these exercises, you should pay special attention to the psychology and common sense approaches to contemplations so that they will have a maximum impact on transforming the life of each exercitant. Not uncommonly, an exercitant may be intently focused on the process of contemplation itself or on the gospel subject matter to the exclusion of other considerations. The observant director looks carefully at all these aspects in order to assess the spiritual and human dynamic at work.

For example, Ignatius is concerned with deepening the contemplations during Phase Two by a singleminded concentration on the subject matter of the week under consideration **[127]** putting aside every other, however green the grass on the other side of the fence may be. Prudential judgments are called for in developing systematic prayer periods so as to lay a basis for a continuing life of prayer **[128]** beyond the favorable "sheltered" time of the retreat, and so as to adapt the number of prayer periods to one's health, age, occupation, and other considerations **[129–130]**.

Ignatius is also concerned that the exercitant prepare simply but reverentially for the prayer periods by the proper "warm up" so that they may be most fruitful **[131]**. Additionally, over and above the norms of Phase One, the director will strive to be alert to the more subtle guidance in the Rules for the Greater Discernment of Spirits, especially those for Phase Two **[328–336]**. These "guidelines are meant to be helpful in understanding the interior movements, especially consolation and spurious consolation, because commonly in the progress of a good person's life the direction of all movements appears to be toward God" and thus the differences between the useful and the useless can be more subtle. We are reminded by Paul in his letter to the Romans of the life-giving, dynamic assistance of the Holy Spirit as we attempt to fulfil our desire to know Jesus more intimately and love him more ardently. We on our part, whether as directors or retreatants, are urged to keep listening to the Holy Spirit with attentive discernment.

PMWYS
pp. 54–55

V. *PHASE TWO OF THE EXERCISES: WEEKS 6 TO 16*

In Phase Two the exercitant focuses on totally immersing himself in contemplation of "the life of our Lord Jesus Christ up to and including Palm Sunday" **[4]**. That is, he places his whole, entire living self—whether thinking, feeling, or imagining—among those involved in these biblical mysteries. This Phase is fundamental for understanding the dynamic of the entire *Spiritual Exercises* since it consists of "several specifically Ignatian exercises" (Egan, 1987, p. 100). The preceding Week 5 exercises that center on the Kingdom of Christ **[91–98]**, and that I place in a transition week, are also specifically Ignatian. In fact, a simple analysis reveals that "The Kingdom of Christ" exercise makes explicit the implicit Christocentrism of the Principle and Foundation already considered in Week 2 because it 'helps us to contemplate the life of the Eternal King' **[91]** and sets the entire Christocentric tone for the second, third and fourth" phases (Egan, 1987, p. 101).

A. A Perspective on the first three weeks of the Phase Two Prayers.

Ignatius suggests a sequential series of, and systematic rules for, and meditations during these first weeks of Phase Two as likely to be most beneficial for the exercitant: the Incarnation—Week 6 **[101–109 & 262]**, the Birth of Jesus—also Week 6 **[110–131 & 264–265]**, and the Hidden Life of Jesus—Weeks 7 & 8 **[266–272]**. David Fleming explains this well: "The grace consistently desired is 'to know Jesus more intimately so that I can love him more and follow him more closely.' The colloquies tend to sharpen that perspective and thus increase one's desire to be "placed" in the particular mystery of Christ's life which has provided the matter for prayer.

....

"It is by means of this style of contemplative prayer that Ignatius has discovered a way for the exercitant to imbibe Jesus' attitudes and approaches to God, to men and women, and to his world. The more we enter into gospel contemplation, the more we heighten the connaturality of our own way of living with the way that Christ lives. By the grace we seek and by the prayer-method we use, we find ourselves drinking in the experiences of

PMWYS pp. 77–82

Jesus, so that we begin to assimilate his values, his loves, his freedom. This style of praying provides the necessary context of decision-making or discernment which forms an essential part of Phase Two and is meant to be an abiding feature of a Christian's life that is shaped by the *Exercises*" (Fleming, 1983, pp. 9–11).

B. Week 9: The Strategy of Jesus

This week in Phase Two follows the Guidelines in which Ignatius deals with the "Two Leaders" and their Strategies—called in the Autograph the "Two Standards" **[136–146]**. This uniquely Ignatian meditation is placed in and logically "forms a tight unity with the Kingdom meditation' . . . The exercitant must focus upon Christ's call to participate in the worldwide work of redemption. The poverty, scorn, and humiliation expected under Christ's 'standard'" [or flag] "are contrasted with the riches, worldly honors, and pride of Satan's 'standard.' Ignatius . . . views life as a battleground between the forces of good and evil. Moreover, the Two Standards exercise is a dramatic presentation of Ignatius' well-known 'Rules for the Discernment of Spirits' **[313–336]**. Here the exercitant asks for basic discernment, "a knowledge of the deceits of the evil chieftain [Satan] . . . and a knowledge of the true life" **[139]** (Egan, 1987, p. 101).

PMWYS *pp. 50–52*

As director you may appreciate a modified approach to Ignatius' Two Standards as it is outlined in the two considerations for Week 5 in "Christ the Eternal King and his Call." Or you may chose to use "Mankind's evolving noosphere" as adapted for Day 3 of Week 7, from Teilhard de Chardin's *The Divine Milieu.* Teilhard uses images based on passages from St. Paul that emphasize the call of each individual to share in the cosmic recreation of the Universe by participating in "building the Earth" with the works of mind and heart. In effect, these works make up Earth's new shell or sphere—Teilhard's noosphere. Teilhard does not use battlefield images; he offers the exercitant an opportunity to call fire (of love) down on the earth, and thus participate in the glorious adventure of building the Kingdom of Christ.

PMWYS *pp. 65–66*

1. What are the qualities of Jesus, our Leader?

Jesus' qualities of character and his strategy shine out in every event of his life, especially as experienced in the meditations of Weeks 5 through 16. However, after we review the prelude to the ministry of Jesus in Mark's "Good News" (Mk, Ch. 1) we meet him as a teacher with authority and as a healer who drew the sick, possessed, and needy to himself "from everywhere." These five closely related accounts of his Galilean ministry tell us much about the moral values of our Leader and the risks he is willing to take to sustain those values. We soon see that Jesus did not hold back even though he knew that his work on behalf of the needy would draw the scrutinizing attention and action-oriented anger of the Scribes and Pharisees. (Mk 2:1–27 & 3: 1–6)

Although these gospel narratives are not specifically addressed in the text of *Place Me With Your Son*, you as director may want to use them to illustrate Jesus' leadership qualities. Meditation on these will enable each exercitant to ask: "How oriented am I to spontaneously help those in need if it will be costly to me in one way or another? Will I act without counting the cost to myself? Was Jesus aware of what the cost of his care for the needy would be to himself? What is that to me?" For dramatic, real life illustrations of these principles from behind the former "Iron Curtain" read *Faith Under Fire and the Revolution in Eastern Europe* (Hedberg, 1992).

2. ***What is the strategy of Jesus, our Leader?***

The broad outline of his strategy is surely revealed in the pages of Scripture and clarified by Jesus in each of his kind and caring cures. However, the blueprint for a strategy in the life of each of us must be discerned and adapted as life unfolds. And, in spite of some formidable obstacles to his intention to follow Christ, Ignatius was so inspired by the strategy of Jesus that he learned what to look for and how to successfully overcome them, and thus eventually came to have an impact of vast proportions on the world's people. One or more of your exercitants may be likewise fired with an overwhelming love of Jesus that will similarly serve to build Christ's Kingdom in unprecedented ways. Ignatius asks us to make use of consolation and desolation, a tried and true method that grew out of his own experiences. This is a powerful way to discern from the very core of our being what is right and what is wrong, especially when we earnestly beg for insight in the quadruple colloquy.

PMWYS *pp. 77–82*

In human warfare the victory, more often than not, is in the hands of whichever leader can outmaneuver the other by deception. This is the tactic of the Evil Spirit. Jesus' tactic is to conquer instead by authenticity, by the power of truth, and by the power of love. His strategy for bringing his Kingdom to fulfillment is to prepare his followers to develop that same kind of genuine spirituality and to prayerfully examine the stuff of daily life—helping them to see the real persons around and to hear what they are actually saying and to observe what they are doing and what they need **[122–125]**. The more deeply your exercitants enter into gospel contemplation of this kind, the more they will find themselves "drinking in the experiences of Jesus and so that [they] begin to and assimilate his values, his loves, and his freedom. This style of contemplative praying provides the necessary context [for] decision-making or discernment" that, as an integral exercise of Phase Two, leads in turn to wise value choices or the "election" **[175–189]**. (Fleming, 1973, pp. 9–10).

PMWYS p. 54

C. *Week 10: The Mission Begins*

PMWYS pp. 83–86

For the rest of Phase Two the exercitants reflect on the call to high adventure, the very same adventure to which the Father called Jesus. In these Exercises for contemplating the public life and mission of Jesus, Ignatius asks each exercitant to to use all five senses in the [Quadruple] COLLOQUY and to focus prayerfully on the GRACE that is as earnestly sought as the prize pearl: ***"The grace will always be to know Jesus more intimately, to love him more intensely and to follow him more closely."***

In all the contemplations on the public life of Jesus, that colloquy is the one described in the meditation on "The Two Leaders and Two Strategies" (sometimes called "The Two Standards") **[147]** and repeated in the meditation on "The Three Classes" **[156–57]**. Further directions are given in **[159]** and **[160]** of the *Exercises*. Thus, the colloquy appropriate for all the prayer contemplations on the public life of Jesus is the fourfold one in which we beg the grace to be received under the Standard of Christ, first in the highest spiritual poverty, and even in actual poverty and insults, if that be God's will"—that is, placed with His Son. See also "Week 10: The Mission Begins" in *Place Me With Your Son* for a perspective on this concept.

PMWYS pp. 83–87

1. The Quadruple Colloquy—a petition by the Exercitant to be placed under Jesus' Banner [Standard].

"Because of the importance of coming to some understanding of the opposing forces of these two leaders [Christ and Satan] and their strategies." [The exercitant above all needs to enter] "into the intensity of the prayer by addressing Mary, Christ, the Holy Spirit, "and the Father and begging favors from them" **[147M]**. Note that in the first part of this colloquy, **[147a]** Ignatius urges the exercitant, in the spirit of the exalted third degree of humility, to "First approach our Lady, asking her to obtain for me from her Son the grace-gift to be his apostle—following him in the highest spiritual poverty, and should God be pleased thereby and want to choose and accept me, even in actual poverty. Even greater is the gift I seek in being able to bear the insults and the contempt of my world, so imitating Christ my Lord ever more closely, provided only I can suffer these without sin on the part of another and without any offense to God" (Fleming, 1978, p.89).

To be repeated later, this colloquy is a severe obstacle for most exercitants even though Ignatius provides several conditions, such as leaving it up to God whether he chooses to accept one for that role **[156–157]**. At the end, two other qualifying provisions are voiced, namely [to receive such a gift only] if there is no sin on the part of another and [if it comes] without offense to God. It appears that Ignatius is seeking from the exercitant such a high degree of generosity and reckless, self-transcending love of Jesus that it will impel such a person to pray diligently to be accepted for a self-sacrificing role like that of Jesus himself.

Ignatius himself, in writing the *Spiritual Exercises* and in directing them, encountered such severe opposition to and misunderstanding of his theology that he was under constant scrutiny and criticism. He even had to bear the stigma of having his spiritual teaching seriously misunderstood, with the result that he was labelled heretical for a time by some theologians called on to evaluate his orthodoxy. In these situations, encountered more than once, Ignatius faced the ultimate kind of "poverty," namely the prospect of being silenced by the very Church that he wanted to serve in such a distinctive way. Given that he actually found himself suffering not only misunderstandings but the threat of being silenced or the enduring of other Inquisition penalties, his colloquy in the context of The Two Standards has the strong sense of immediacy that may not face your exercitants, living today in a somewhat more benign theological climate. "This colloquy echoes Ignatius' La Storta vision wherein he experienced mystically the Father placing him with the Son. It also summarizes many elements in Ignatius' trinitarian and mediator mysticisms" (Egan, 1987, p. 101). If you are familiar with the extreme misunderstanding and opposition of many Church authorities to the far-sighted ideas of Teilhard de Chardin, you may remind the exercitants that he remained loyal to the Church in spite of extreme provocation and personal anguish. Indeed, much of the primary document of Vatican II is replete with phrases from the writings of Teilhard. Recall too, that *Lumen Gentium* was written less than a decade after the death of Teilhard who had been exiled to North America in the early 1950s for his "dangerous teachings."

2. The "Three Types of Persons" who respond.

Ignatius envisions that three types of persons may respond with greater or lesser generosity to the call and strategy of Jesus **[149–155]**. "This is a meditation . . . to aid me in my freedom of choice according to God's call to me" **[149]**. The grace that Ignatius proposes is "to ask grace to choose what is more to the glory of His Divine Majesty and the salvation of my soul" or as Fleming reads it, "I ask that I may be free enough to choose whatever the lead of God's grace may indicate as his particular call to me" (**[152]**, Fleming, pp. 92–93).

The supposition presented to the exercitant by Ignatius is that each of the three types of persons has quite a few possessions—not always acquired with the best of motives and, in fact, sometimes quite selfishly. Yet "in general, each is a good person, and he would like to serve God, even to the extent that if these possessions were to come in the way of his salvation, he would like to be free of them" **[150–151]**.

The First Type of person is obviously "a lot of talk, but no action" **[153]**, and the Second Type is ready "to do everything but the one thing necessary" **[154]**. The Third Type is characterized as saying "to do Your will is my desire" **[155]**. Ignatius develops the description of each type so graphically that each exercitant may recognize where she stands in the "effort to be in balance, ready to move in any direction that the call from God may take her. In *Choosing Christ in the World,* the presentation of these good but different persons in a credible fantasy helps to contemporize the dilemma faced by each of Three Couples (Tetlow, 1989, p. 161).

Recognizing that an exercitant "may discover some attachment opposed to actual poverty or a repugnance to it, or . . . not indifferent to poverty and riches," Ignatius urges drastic counteraction or *"agere contra."* Literally it means "to act against" a recognizable tendency or repugnance and is sometimes referred to as "self denial." In the spirit of *agere contra,* Ignatius further urges all exercitants "to come to Jesus our Lord in prayer and beg him to choose us to serve him in actual poverty. We should beg with a certain insistence, and we should plead for it—***but always wanting what God wants for us.***" **[157]**.

3. The "Three Kinds of Humility" propose three levels of commitment.

The culmination of Phase Four, the final stage of the Exercises, is the "Contemplation to Gain Love." The literal translation by Mullan from the Autograph is gloriously simple and astonishingly comprehensive: "Note. First, it is well to remark two things: the first is that love ought to be put more in deeds than in words.

"The second, love consists in interchange between the two parties; that is to say, in the lover's giving and communicating to the beloved what he has or out of what he has or can; and so, on the contrary, the beloved to the lover. So that if the one has knowledge, he gives to the one who has it not. The same of honors, of riches; and so the one to the other." **[230]**

And, of course, the level of love that each exercitant can give and receive at this point depends in the last analysis on the kind of humility attained—in other words, on the depth and range of commitment to the authentic imitation of Christ.

"Humility lies in the acceptance of Jesus Christ as the fullness of what it means to be human. To be humble is to live as close to the truth as possible: that I am created to the likeness of Christ, that I am meant to live according to the pattern of his paschal mystery, and that my whole fulfillment is found in being as near to Christ as he draws me to himself" (Fleming, 1978, p. 101).

A most endearing virtue, humility's practice by most of us places it on the "endangered species" list. Nevertheless, Ignatius describes three progressively more excellent kinds of humility and proposes them for all exercitants **[165–168]**.

As director, you will help them remember and understand that humility is about love of another over self—it is about self transcendence. The first two kinds of humility are about a certain level of love, but love that is infused with a strong element of obedience. The third kind of humility, at a most exalted level, is a sheer gift of God's grace, an act of perfect love. It would seem that only those who embrace the third kind of humility can attain the fullness of divine love.

a. "The First Kind of Humility. This is living out the truth which is necessary for salvation, and so it describes one extreme of the spectrum. **[165]** I would want to do nothing that would cut me off from God—not even were I made head of all creation or even just to save my own life here on earth. I know that grave sin in this sense is to miss the whole meaning of being a person—one who is created and redeemed and is destined to live forever in love with God my Creator and Lord" (Fleming, 1978, p. 101).

b. "The Second Kind of Humility. This is more demanding than the first, and so we find ourselves somewhere along the middle of the spectrum. **[166]** My life is firmly grounded in the fact that the reality of being a person is seen fully in Jesus Christ. Just as 'I have come to do your will, O God' is the motivating force of his life, so the only real principle of choice in my life is to seek out and do the will of my Father. With this habitual attitude, I find that I can maintain a certain balance in my inclinations to have riches rather than poverty, honor rather than dishonor, or to desire a long life rather than a short life. I would not want to turn away from God even in small ways, because my whole desire is to respond ever more faithfully to his call" (Fleming, 1978, p. 101).

c. "The Third Kind of Humility. This is close to the other end of the spectrum, since it demands the understanding and action of a greater grace-gift. **[167]** It consists in this—I so much want the truth of Christ's life to be fully the truth of my own that I find myself, moved by grace, with a love and a desire for poverty in order to be with the poor Christ; a love and a desire for insults in order to be closer to Christ in his own rejection by people; a love and a desire to be considered worthless and a fool for Christ, rather than to be esteemed as wise and prudent according to the standards of the world. By grace, I find myself so moved to follow Jesus Christ in the most intimate union possible, that his experiences are reflected in my own. In that, I find my delight" (Fleming, 1978. pp. 101 & 103).

If the exercitant wishes "to move more in the direction of this third kind of humility, it will be help much to make use of the [fourfold] colloquy, as it has been explained above" **[157]**. Ignatius suggests that an exercitant should beg with a certain insistence that our Lord choose one for the gift of this third kind of humility in order to find one's own life patterned according to Jesus—"but always, of course, if this be for the greater praise and service of God" **[168]** (Fleming, 1978, p. 103).

What director and exercitants must recognize is that each of these degrees of humility represents a high degree of spirituality, each progressively higher than the other. To live the third degree represents the most ardent kind of self-transcending love, a gratuitous gift of such magnitude yet generating such repugnance initially that only perfect love can seek it. Only one who "thinks as God thinks" can even feel the desire to desire to be given this gift of complete freedom from self concern and of perfect love of Jesus.

4. Authentic Humility as Degrees of True Freedom.

This is a good place for you as director to discuss freedom—true freedom, not only through poverty in terms of possessions, but also in terms of the extreme of poverty. In asking the exercitant to reflect on what (s)he cannot live without, it will become clear that although we Americans prize "freedom" as a symbol of all that is best about our country, we may actually enjoy relatively little authentic freedom—if we are fettered by perceived needs of every kind. Radical freedom comes from humility, and the greatest possible freedom is to be had if we are granted the gift of the Third Type of Humility, freedom from every kind of fear and loss.

Poverty is often thought of in terms of the lack of money for daily needs and the absence of security from deprivation. Nevertheless, we all realize that the loss of reputation, such as Jesus experienced when he was "tried" and crucified as a criminal, is the most severe form of poverty. In trying to imagine the Third Degree of Humility in the concrete circumstances of life one can simply ask what impoverishment could be greater than to be convicted of a crime that one did not commit. One can imagine also the deep and rancorous sense of loss deep within those innocent persons who have been publicly but wrongfully accused of rape, whoring, pederasty, or any heinous crimes, and who thereby have lost their greatest possession, their good reputation. Moreover, such actual impoverishment often is exacerbated because the "victim" who experiences extreme poverty of this kind is commonly robbed also of confidence and self esteem, and is thus prevented from recovery from that poverty. It seems more than likely that there are many who have been wrongfully imprisoned or punished thus throughout history. The wrongful trial and execution of Our Lord is, of course, a most shocking example of such cruelly imposed and absolute impoverishment. As director, you may need to remind each exercitant that for Jesus, as it would have been for us in his circumstances, the outcome of this shame-filled circumstance was envisioned more by faith than by foreknowledge.

D. Week 11: Jesus Calls Me by Name

PMWYS *pp. 87–92*

The dynamic of this week is very powerful. By the quality of what happens in prayer during this week you as director may generally judge if, on average, the members of the group have been able to set aside sufficient time for meditative prayer. By placing themselves among those Jesus calls by name—Peter, Zaccheus, Lazarus, and the others—each exercitant's hearing of that personal call cannot help but make a indelible impression. Indeed, some may even hear and experience a vivid and unexpected new name that they feel Jesus is using to call to them.

At this point in one of our recent Boston College retreats, an exercitant was ill and temporarily absent. So the group sent him a sheet of paper folded like a card with a brief word from each.

One wrote "I miss your gentle presence." At the next meeting he shared with the group the fact that some friends tease him affectionately by calling him "Gentle Ken." But he acknowledged that it is a name that expresses what he feels called to live out, yet a role in which he feels that he is taken advantage of from time to time. At such times he told us that he rebels and goes into soul searching about whether he should or should not be more aggressive and set limits to his "taken for granted" generosity with his time and his availability. For him or for any such a person to reach a proper balance, it is useful to help him weigh prayerfully the pluses and minuses of any concrete situation wherein one wants to be free of compulsions or of wrong burdens, whether self-imposed or imposed by others.

1. Honest Reactions Help Reluctant Exercitants.

Another time an exercitant, in meditating on the gift sought confessed to our group that she was repulsed by the thought of "serving him . . . in the highest poverty and contempt if that be his will." This is a common reaction and one that the exercitants may often feel guilty about. They should be reassured that this is an inevitable reaction by people who are being realistic and honest. Moreover, the reactions of resentment and guilt may both serve to set up a dynamic and beneficial tension that will help in the continuing discernment of one's growth in generous response to the Lord. For example, a "Gentle Ken," after exercising true discernment, may conclude that expressing gentle and generous solidarity with those in pain and suffering is an appropriate response to such needs. Yet such generosity takes a toll because some regard it as weakness and thus a character flaw. His conscious discernment tells him otherwise, but it may be done at the price of a friend's admiration. To that extent then he is serving Jesus and his people in silently accepting a bit of "contempt" from those from whom he otherwise hopes for admiration. Such sincere expression and private soul searching can generate a concrete resolution that ultimately leads to peace of mind even though it is a response to what in the abstract seems only a repulsive call to the third degree of humility.

2. The "Call Outs" Make the Meditations Personal.

During Week 11 several passages in the Gospels offer meditations that deal with specifically named persons, including Zaccheus, Peter, Lazarus, and even Jesus himself. Most exercitants find the meditations of this week very personalized and relate strongly to the "call out" by name, especially of those whose attitudes or circumstances parallel theirs. Zaccheus really wanted to get a good hard look at Jesus, for instance, so he could find out what Jesus seemed to be like. But he was also short, so in a burst of unashamed enthusiasm he sprinted ahead in order to climb a tall tree along Jesus' route. And he climbed the tree—rather an unsophisticated act for the chief tax collector and a wealthy man. Busy as he was with the crowd, Jesus recognized something special in Zaccheus because he addressed him by name and told him to hurry down out of that tree. Then, in front of the crowd he explained why: "I mean to stay at your house today." The Gospel says that Zaccheus descended quickly and welcomed Jesus with delight. But the crowd did not; he was a known sinner. Nevertheless, we can logically ask: Why shouldn't such enthusiastic simplicity and sincere readiness to repent please Jesus? This seems so because Zaccheus backed up his good intentions by unhesitatingly admitting that he was a sinner and would pay back fourfold anyone he had defrauded. Moreover, Jesus responded to the fact of the crowd's hostility to Zaccheus as a recognized sinner by pointing out that Zaccheus, being a descendant of Abraham was, as we are, one of the lost sheep that the Good Shepherd comes looking for: "Today salvation has come to your house." We too must all recognize that we are offspring of Abraham and that the Good Shepherd comes seeking to stay at "our house" in order to bring us salvation.

E. *Week 12: Jesus Teaches Me with Words of "Power and Light"*

The meditations of this part of Phase Two in the retreat are focused on the meaning of Christ's Kingdom as expressed in his words of power and light. The Sermon on the Mount is that summation (Mt 5: 1:48). Ignatius places the *PRELUDE* for what he calls *"MAKING ELECTION"* or what Fleming calls *"INTRODUCTION TO MAKING A CHOICE OF A STATE OR WAY OF LIFE"* **[169]** immediately after the annotations on *THREE KINDS OF HUMILITY* **[165–168]**. The basic information and alternatives for making a choice, or for arriving at a decision, as well as a treatment of typical subject matter of such decisions and choices are throughout these guidelines **[169–174]**. Ignatius' guiding principle deciding on a course of action is that "only one thing is really important—to seek and find what God calls me to at this time in my life."

PMWYS *pp. 93–97*

Stressing the significance of that principle, Ignatius later added to his instructions: "During the exercises of the Election, the exercitant should not direct his attention simply to the movement of spirits going on within him (that is by discerning the fluctuations of consolation and desolation), but rather to the love of God which both precedes and accompanies all movements of the soul—and he will do this by continuing to contemplate the mysteries of the life of Christ." (Rahner, 1968, p. 146). And, as Rahner noted, Ignatius explicitly repeated in the Directory that by attending to the movement of spirits within the heart (discerning one's own consolation and desolation mood swings), one can honestly learn and feel the will of God.

PMWYS
p. 93

Throughout this week various matters related to **"Election"** are raised by Ignatius and these include the following four considerations:

1. Introduction to Making a Choice (or Election) of a State or Way of Life.

In this twelfth week the exercitant becomes aware more so than previously of the "Election" to be made. The Guidelines become important in order to get a better idea of the meaning of the choice or election in the concrete. **[169]**

The election is commonly taken to indicate a major clear-cut choice to be made. However true that may be as a concept, I believe that it needs to be approached in a less idealistic and more foundational way. For any big decision to be well made and of lasting value, a pattern of ***authenticity*** in decision making with regard to small matters in everyday life must be established. It may be helpful here to consult *What are they saying about Mysticism."* In Chapter 9, "A Future Mysticism," Harvey Egan summarizes Bernard Lonergan's insightful dialogue on science and mysticism, particularly on what they have in common and basically of their universal applicability. In response to the question, "Who is the authentic person? Lonergan answers that the authentic person is the one who is faithful to the transcendental precepts, namely by being attentive, intelligent, reasonable, responsible, and by being in love. A sound spirituality seems hardly possible without one's fidelity to the basic dynamism of the mind responsible for abiding fidelity to these transcendental precepts.

In this part of the retreat the question of whether one may be called to the religious life and/or to the priesthood may surface. This is quite appropriate material for the election at one level of discernment and should not be discouraged. However, at a more foundational level it is mandatory to discern one's authenticity in areas such as one's greatest weakness. However, major decisions like these may be more appropriately addressed incrementally and perhaps more definitively at a later time, or at least later in the retreat.

For example, one may have been long conditioned by the prejudice of one's own convictions to "go along to get along" in a mild mannered way and thus be somewhat distressed to realize that one is, at least subconsciously, living a bit inauthentically to some degree or other. Also, as a result of this all too human failing members of one's own circle of friends or family may have fallen into inappropriate behavior patterns for lack of a good role model. That, for instance, is a sad fact in the case of a weak parent. One may, therefore, need first of all to elect or make choices on a continuing basis in concrete circumstances so as to respond more authentically. This may prompt others to ask "what got into that one?" "Why isn't he as pliable as he used to be? and so forth.

Attention to what might well be "details" may at first be called too trivial for an election. However, I believe that it is impossible to make an election with regard to "big choices" until one's orientation to the "small" and more foundational matters is attended to and a pattern of authentic responses is well established. Often the "baggage" that overloads and holds one back are the inauthentic behavior patterns acquired somewhat passively in childhood and/or later in life and never properly or effectively addressed.

In summary, as one is released more fully from the emotional fetters that bind, one becomes, like Lazarus, unbound and fully alive again. It is possible, for example, to hear and march to one's own drummer rather than to the one being heard by one's parent or one's spouse. Then, the bigger choices will become clearer and the response to one's own drummer can be more enthusiastic and whole hearted without being hurtful to others.

The exercitant should read the following annotations, interweaving relevant considerations into contemplations on the choices made by Matthew when he was called or by Paul when he was offered a chance to turn his life around **[175]**.

2. ***Matters about Which a Choice Should Be Made.***
   - **a.** Lawful and Good Alternatives **[170]**
   - **b.** Permanent Commitments **[171]**
   - **c.** Permanent Commitments already Made **[172]**

3. ***Three Times When a Correct and Good Choice of a State or Way of Life May Be Made.***
   - **a.** First Time **[175]**
   - **b.** Second Time **[176]**

c. Third Time **[177–178]**
   i. First Pattern of Making a Good and Correct Choice **[179–183]**
   ii. Second Pattern of Making a Good and Correct Choice **[184–188]**

4. Some Directions for the Renewal of or Recommitment to a State or Way of Life already Chosen.

"Often in retreat, [one can find oneself] not so much faced with the question of a new decision, but rather with the living out of a choice already made" **[189]**.

PMWYS *pp. 93–96*

Study Ignatius' Annotations [278 & 280] and then the meditations in Matthew's Gospel (Mt 5: 1–48; 6: 1–34; 14: 22–34; & 7: 1–29) as they are presented in the text. These meditations are calculated to nourish the grain of wheat that has lost its life by being buried in the ground, that is to say, in generously lived discipleship. These contemplative prayers are intended to help it grow with life transformed, flourishing to such full discipleship that his Kingdom may thereby come to be for all who are nourished by the new wheat that is the harvest of that death to self. Review also the insightful commentary that stresses the love of God that both precedes and accompanies all movements within the soul (Rahner, 1968, p. 146).

PMWYS *pp. 93–96*

Sometimes the exercitant may tend to think that Ignatius was unduly hard on himself and his exercitants when he asks them to pray for a desire to serve Him and His people in the highest poverty and contempt if that be his will. However, if we turn to Luke's beatitudes he asks no less, especially "Blest shall you be when men hate you, when they ostracize you and insult you and proscribe your name as evil <u>because of the Son of Man</u>. When we find ourselves in concrete circumstances that demand that we be faithful in spite of the dire consequences outlined in The Great Discourse (Lk 6:17–34) or by Matthew in passages cited earlier, then the Holy Spirit gives us enlightenment and strength, "power and light."

In many parts of the world there are those whose situations in life force them to live heroically and self-sacrificially if they are to be authentic Christians. A deeply challenging, significant and beautifully illustrated book, that mainly consists of interviews by Augustin Hedberg, is based on transcripts from the Public Broadcasting Documentary, *Faith Under Fire.* It is the heroic and tragic story of fidelity, compromise, and betrayal on the part of many priests and religious during the six or seven decades before the collapse of Communism in Czechoslovakia and Poland. It also confronts the problems of forgiveness and bitterness after the fall of Communism, and makes us all wonder how strong or weak, how forgiving or how bitter we would be, subjected to these circumstances. Peter was forgiven by Jesus, but was he ever fully forgiven by all of Jesus' disciples?

F. Weeks 13, 14, & 15: Jesus Heals,

The meditations of Week 13 are calculated to increase hope, love, and faith so that the exercitant may be healed and so energized as to be ready to do all that the Father desires. This will come from the realization that the healing ministry of Jesus is also a saving ministry. A recognition of each one's helplessness and an intense desire to be drawn in prayer to Jesus for healing will result in saving of the spirit as well.

PMWYS *pp. 98–101*

A recognition by exercitants of the need for healing will bring them back to the Election. Because an understanding of the movements of consolation and desolation are fundamental to discernment of one's needs, have the exercitants return again to Guidelines **[316–17]**.

Challenges,

Now each exercitant is challenged not only to do "the one thing necessary" for an authentic following of Jesus but also, as a generous follower desiring to offer distinguished service, to be sincerely willing to do the "one thing more." As each exercitant ponders the challenges that these meditations stir within the innermost self, it is important that the guidelines be reviewed so as to improve recognition of the meaning of consolation and desolation.

PMWYS *pp. 102–108*

At this point you, as director, should pay special attention to "what the exercitant really wants and deeply desires." A discerning and experienced spiritual director can at this point be very helpful by consulting with the exercitant who is challenged to make a prayerful response to the call of Jesus, the call to high adventure as a companion of Jesus in seeking the Kingdom, and the desire to share his lot and his suffering.

PMWYS *p. 102*

& Nurtures

In these exercises, your retreatants will contemplate the gentle Christ who welcomes those in need of rest and comfort for their often overburdened selves.

PMWYS *p. 109–113*

PHASE TWO OF THE EXERCISES: WEEKS 6 TO 16

1. Nurturing Love.—The Reality of Jesus.

As the transition from Phase Two to Phase Three approaches, at the end of Week 16, each exercitant's need and desire is to become more aware and convinced of Jesus' passionate concern for her and the concomitant need to accept that nurturing love. In sum, the exercitant both needs and desires to become "more passionate than ever before, in serving him and his people, sharing his lot in poverty and the contempt of others if that is his will." Moreover, by this time the exercitant is coming face-to-face progressively with the reality that each one's life mirrors more and more that of the one who is being intensely loved. These contemplations look intensely at the highly confrontational situations as they increase and ultimately bring down the wrath of the power group in Jerusalem and in turn lead inevitably to the reality of death for Jesus.

2. Sacred Listening—Hearing Others as Jesus did.

PMWYS p. 4

Misunderstandings can be very hard to bear but they can be minimalized if one listens as Jesus listened. Members of one of my retreat groups, in meditating on the gospel narratives in relation to some of their own life situations, focused on the misunderstandings that arise from others being very judgmental and condemnatory, rather than tolerant. Some of what they aired made clear that several were longing for the kind of acceptance enjoyed by those at Cana, or by the Gentile woman who got help for her daughter, or when Jesus met up with the Samaritan woman at the well. Take note also of Ignatius' *praesupponendum* or "plus sign" for directors and exercitants alike, as he explains it early in his text. One exercitant, whose church group had been perceived as being very judgmental and difficult to deal with, recommended a prayerful approach by having the group agree to begin their meeting with a prayer for "listening in community" based on the Episcopalian method of "sacred listening," This approach sounded to me like a variant of what Ignatius instructs us to do: to listen to each other and to prepare to put a favorable interpretation on whatever is being said until and even if the contrary is the only answer perceived. **[22]**

Some of the most difficult wounds to accept in the exchanges of everyday life are "put-downs" and signs of lack of respect and affection of one person for another. On the other hand, acceptance and respect may bind two quite different people together in the bond of friendship and even shared faith. One member of a retreat group, in contemplating the conversation between Jesus and the woman at the well, thought of it as an example of "truth-telling out of a spirit of love and without put-down." Jesus was undoubtedly delighted in her rapid growth in faith him and her public profession of him as the Messiah (Jo 4: 4–42). This in spite of the fact that Jesus left himself vulnerable to criticism and misunderstanding for speaking to a Samaritan. Yet in that "outsider" he recognized great potential for faith. Nevertheless, Jesus engaged in a bit of truth telling after she forthrightly admitted that she had no husband. In his reply "Jesus exclaimed . . . The fact is that you have had five, and the man you are living with now is not your husband." However, it is clear that she took no offense from his reply but used it instead to bolster her faith in him as a prophet. It is clear that Jesus did not engage in "put-downs," least of all with women, and with women who trusted him, as obviously both this woman at the well and the Syrophoenician woman did (Mt 15:21–28). Take note that not one of the women to whom Jesus revealed both himself and the mysteries of God were "wimps." They were strong and their own persons and, as the narratives illustrate, they listened and heard what he had to say. Awareness meditations, such as those from de Mello's *Sadhana,* tend to reinforce the habit of listening and hearing what is really being said. So much of our lives may be spent living either in the past or in the future if we do not pay attention or if we do not live in the present. Our conversations and discussions do take place in the present; however, unless we cultivate being in the present by awareness meditation, it is so easy to hear only a fraction of what others are saying and thus come away with a distorted version of what they are really saying to us.

3. ***What is wanted and desired—the power of Faith in Jesus.***

Over the years gratitude and trust are emotions that have surfaced among several of my retreat groups, especially during the readings in the meditations of Week 15. One step beyond the "plus sign" these look to our being ready to accept another's statement, as the Samaritan woman at the well did, and as the Syrophoenician woman did. Jesus in turn recognized and responded to them—particularly to the admirable intensity of the latter's passionate desire for a cure for her daughter. Many in the groups often found that "letting go" of one's preconceptions is important if one is to really hear what others are saying and/or feeling rather than what one may imagine they are saying—and, as they acknowledged, that is truly "sacred listening." This letting go leads also to distinguishing between "my doing God's work" and "doing the work that God gives me to do."

The former often being what one can choose without much discernment and perhaps permeated by self righteousness, as opposed to discernment-based acceptance of what one may learn to recognize as God's will revealed in day to day fidelity to the path that Jesus invites each of us to walk with him daily.

A reflection that commonly emerges during retreat group discussions, is Jesus' characteristic predilection for the disenfranchised whom he unfailingly championed—especially women. Jesus recognized the great faith exhibited by many women, typically in the context of steadfast, wholehearted trust. In fact, he seems unable to refuse a request prompted by great love such as that shown by the Syrophonecian woman whose love prompted a petition that produced a change of cosmic importance that changed the very timetable Jesus had for offering salvation to the Gentiles.

4. Big and Little Elections—both Significant.

Another retreatant's reflection that emerged from this same rather rich session relates to what the election was that God was calling him to—namely to root out unworthy, ingrained habits of speech using four letter words. He honestly came to see the election not so much as "cleaning up my mouth as cleaning up my heart." This all too common fault, by the way, is typically regarded as trivial. But it may often signify chronic impatience and a somewhat unattractive and irreverent response to life's inevitable irritants which, with a change of attitude, can and do become prayer. It is another aspect of the "plus sign" occasions which can both strengthen one's patience with the slow and the thoughtless, and facilitate acceptance of a splinter from the cross, so to speak.

5. The Marriage Feast of Cana—the "beginning of the messianic age."

PMWYS
pp. 109–10

Because of its messianic symbolism we need to review certain aspects of the Marriage Feast of Cana. In addition to perspectives thus noted, there are other treasures in this narrative of Jesus' first public appearance. The evangelist begins his "sign" theology with this account: Jesus did this as the beginning of his signs" (John 2:11). The meaning of this sign is manifold as one perceptive commentator realizes, but focuses on: "the arrival through Jesus of the messianic age. What is changed in this incident is not simply water, but water for Old Testament ceremonial washings. It is changed not simply into wine, but into wine of highest quality and of surprising quantity. . . . Such a superabundance of wine was a frequent prophetic figure of speech for the dawning of the messianic age (Amos 9:13–14; Joel

3:18). . . . Consequently changing Old Testament water into messianic wine, signifies or signs, for John and for all, the passing of the old into the new. The messianic era has arrived. The feast symbolizes the messianic banquet. And the messianic bridegroom, he who supplies the wine, is Jesus himself (John 3:29). The allusion to the hour of Jesus' death in verse 4 may even mean that John wants his audience to think also of *the* messianic wine that will be the result and Eucharistic sacrament of Jesus' death" (Flanagan, 1989, CBC, p. 984).

WEEK 16: JESUS BOTH ACCEPTS & BESTOWS LOVE

6. The Father's Will, God's Glory, and God's Manifested Presence.

The troublesome, apparently out-of-order remark by Jesus in Verse 4: "Woman, how does your concern affect me? My hour has not yet come," was apparently selected by John who used the story for new beginnings. He appears to have inserted verse 4 "to affirm, as do the other Gospels, that during Jesus' public life, until his hour came, his work was determined solely by the Father's will" (Flanagan, 1989, CBC, p. 984). How appropriate a model for us other sons and daughters of such a Father.

John also made use of "this story to initiate his theology of glory, 'and so revealed his glory'" (v.11). Most à propos to this stage of the retreat, John's view of glory holds that glory is "God's *manifested presence.* God glorifies us when he manifests himself in us; we glorify him when we manifest him to the world. In this instance at Cana, God's presence is manifested in his Son, his Revealer" (Flanagan, 1989, p. 984).

G. *Week 16: Jesus Both Accepts and Bestows Love*

The contemplations of this week on the public ministry of Jesus bring to a close the Exercises of Phase Two. Then the transition from Phase Two to Phase Three will take us to a kind of threshold—not only for Jesus but also for all of his followers, ourselves included. I can only reiterate what I say in the text for that week: "It was the well-founded belief of Ignatius that contemplations of Jesus carrying out his Father's mission to bring forgiveness and salvation to a sinful world would inspire faith and love—love strong enough to face the cross that always cast its shadow over the landscape of the terrain that Jesus trod. Only love built on faith will be strong enough to accept—yes, even to embrace—the cross as the price to pay for bringing his message and salvation to those to whom we, his disciples, are sent."

PMWYS *pp. 114–118*

PMWYS *pp. 114*

PHASE TWO OF THE EXERCISES: WEEKS 6 TO 16

During this week each exercitant is urged to beg the Lord for the gift of the third degree of humility in order that everyday life may be patterned on that of Jesus, provided that this be for the greater praise and service of God. Contemplations to foster this high degree of generosity, even reckless abandon, focus on three signs—the first, the anointing of the feet of Jesus by Mary (the final episode in the "Book of Signs" and done sincerely by the Magdalen in spite of the cynical comments of the mean spirited); the second, the cure of the man born blind whose strong-hearted belief allowed him to stand up to the establishment bullies; and the third, the final day of the public ministry of Jesus and his final, triumphant entry into Jerusalem.

VI. PREPARATION FOR PHASE THREE PRAYER

A. The contrast between the purposes of the Retreat's Phase Two and Phase Three Contemplations

"The central point of" Phase Three "is the great mystery of the close union between the suffering Christ and the exercitant" (Peters, 1968, p. 134). The concentration upon the suffering Jesus and upon one's compassion here and now with him is vital to the exercitant's involvement in the Passion" (Stanley, 1986, p. 203).

At this point, the director should ask the exercitants to review the "Preparation for Phase Three Prayer," very carefully. Ignatius asks each exercitant to note that besides the three guidelines of Phase Two—seeing the persons, hearing what they are saying, and observing what they are doing **[106, 107, 108]**—he is introducing three additional guidelines to help achieve the goals of Phase Three. These are at the core of the power of Phase Three of the Spiritual Exercises **[195, 196, & 197]**.

PMWYS pp. 119–22

In the contemporary "parallel" reading these guidelines are succinctly summarized: "In addition, during this [Phase Three], I should make even greater effort to labor with Christ through all his anguish, his struggle, his suffering, or what he desires to suffer. At the time of the Passion, I should pay special attention to how the divinity hides itself so that Jesus seems so utterly human and helpless. To realize that Christ loves me so much that he willingly suffers everything for my rejections and sins makes me ask: What can I, in response, do for him?" (Fleming, 1980, p. 117).

Also, remind the exercitants to prayerfully read again all the appropriate annotations in the text, and then with your help as director, to reflect on the strategy that prompted Ignatius to develop these guidelines in the first place. Additionally, Ignatius makes it clear that the exercitant can only be deeply affected by the mysteries of the Lord's passion and death if he enters heart and soul into them and be single-minded in contemplating them **[206]**.

1. The contemplations of Phase Three place us in the everyday renewal of the Passion.

As you will see, Ignatius makes a radical change in strategy during Phase Three. The first followers of Jesus, recalling these events hour by hour and place by place, set them down in great

PMWYS p. 119

detail. Ignatius urges the exercitant to do likewise, "watching and praying with Him in his agony, conscious too that his passion is reenacted daily in the body of His poor and suffering people.

Emphasize to your group that in the course of Phase Three contemplations it may become very obvious to them that the disciples and especially Simon Peter failed woefully not only the test of the third degree of humility, but almost every other test—except that they did not despair of Jesus' love. They knew they wanted to be his disciples but they were afraid and confused, but not so dispirited that they gave up totally to become irrevocably dispersed. Later (in Phase Four) the exercitants will look at Jesus' response to all these weaknesses and failures during the disciples' incredible reunion and reconciliation with a hate-free Jesus.

2. The Colloquy—intensified now and enlarged so as to unite us daily with the living Christ.

PMWYS *pp. 120–21*

Now, have the exercitants read and review some aspects of the activity that Ignatius refers to as "Colloquy." The Colloquy should basically be an intimate conversation between friends. In fact, words may become superfluous at times—times that may "include the depth of feeling, love, and compassion, which allows us just *to be there.*" At other times the appropriate words may well up from heartfelt recesses in the depth of one's being. Selected readings appropriate for leading into Phase Three themes will include those from both the Old and New Testament (Is. 43: 16–21; Ps. 126: 1–6; Philip.3:8–14; Jo. 8:1–11). The conspicuous motif is that faith in Jesus is our only justice. Indeed, we see that it is only because of Jesus' love for us, that we can rise out of our slavery, out of our Babylon in which we have been taken captive, even though we are sinners and are frightened and weak.

Certainly Paul's understanding of Jesus changed his whole value system and it can change that of an exercitant. "I have come to rate all as loss in the light of the surpassing knowledge of my Lord Jesus Christ. For his sake I have forfeited everything. I have accounted all else as rubbish so that Christ may be my wealth and I may be in him. . . . I wish to know Christ and the power flowing from his resurrection, likewise to know how to share in his sufferings by being formed into the pattern of his death. Thus do I hope that I may arrive at resurrection from the dead. . . .—life on high in Jesus Christ." (Phil. 3:8–14). In effect, as Martin Luther King put it, if one does not feel so strongly about something or someone so as to be willing to die for it, then one is already dead and life is really not worth living.

B. Transition from Phase Two to Phase Three

TRANSITION FROM PHASE TWO TO PHASE THREE

The nature of the transition from Phase Two to Phase Three is made clear not only in the subject matter for meditation but most especially in the attitude of Jesus in the difficult times of his life and death, his time of diminishment—the model for each exercitant's own attitudes.

1. The shadow of the Cross falls also on Christ's followers.

As each exercitant turns away from Jericho with Jesus and accompanies him south on the dusty trek to Jerusalem, the shadow of the Cross falls over the landscape. What form that cross may take the exercitant cannot ordinarily know, but it is part of her destiny and will be the principal secret of her apostolic success as a contemplative in action. Early in the history of the church one of the popes took as a title for himself and his successors "servant of the servants of the Lord." This is a title that both Ignatius and the exercitants should be able to relate to as each considers that one's function is that of one whose life's fulfillment and glory is to serve the followers of Christ and to do all that may enable true union with God. In these readings, especially in Matthew's last discourse, our Lord's idea is clearly presented, namely that as a follower of Christ, one's association with him is not to be like that in civil societies where the one in charge all too often "lords it over" the others (Mt. 6:20).

2. "Whoever would rank first among you must serve the needs of all."

Among his followers, whoever is at the head must serve the rest, not seek to be served—a difficult ideal in practice. The temptation to use authority for self is so strong that one can easily become cynical, especially in church- or religion-based societies. Zebedee's mother thought she was doing the right thing in seeking the exclusive places of honor for "her boys," even though she should have known that the other disciples would be furious with her and with them. Jesus puts that "presumptuous" exercise of power and ambition into perspective, "It cannot be like that with you. Anyone among you who aspires to greatness must serve the rest, and whoever wants to rank first among you must serve the needs of all. Such is the case with the Son of Man who has come, not to be served by others, but to serve, to give his own life as a ransom for the many."

3. To be desired—To follow wherever He may lead.

The appropriate attitude as the exercitants enter Phase Three should not be that we desire to suffer in any one of a variety of ways—that is foolishness. The attitude that should be prayed for is developed and conditioned by the desire to follow wherever Jesus is calling each exercitant to go, even to a new Jerusalem. And the exercitant is prepared to take on, like him, whatever life burdens and suffering may go with that "deal." Suffering may be seen either as a means to an end, or as a good accompaniment to satisfying labor for the Kingdom. Jesus did not embrace the cross for pain's sake but for his Father's sake—as something that was his Father's will. The exercitant's same acceptance of any necessary cross must take place incrementally, step by step as required by reason of each life and each life's work, and as that work is revealed—that is, whether that work is active or passive, and whether growth or diminishment. Teilhard de Chardin has eloquently addressed our participation in building the Kingdom of Christ both in "The Divinization of our Activities" and in "The Divinization of our Passivities" (Teilhard de Chardin, 1960, pp. 49–94).

The desire of the just completed Second Phase, has been and is "'for an intimate knowledge of Jesus in order that I may love him more and follow him more closely.' We seek to know his values, his loves, his hates, his dreams, his hopes. We want to know what is in his heart so that we might be so much in love with him that nothing, not even our fear of suffering and of death, will get in the way of following him. As we are given the grace of this Phase, "we find ourselves more and more focused on Jesus, less and less on ourselves. . . . those who have the desire of [the Second Phase] "are gradually freed of enough of their self-centeredness . . . that Jesus does become the love of their lives, their closest friend, their dearest companion. As they come to the end of this stage of their spiritual journey, they—like Bartimaeus after he receives his sight—want to follow Jesus along the road (Mt 10:52), even if the road should be the Way of the Cross. They are ready to begin the Third Week" (Barry, March 9, 1992 letter, p. 1).

Reviewing Mark's "good news" shows us how well he prepares his Christian followers for the ultimate conflict of Jesus life—and, in turn, prepares them for their own "ultimates," and each exercitant for his (Mk 2–3). He later suggests that the same treatment Jesus endured can be expected by those who follow "the Son of Man." (Mk. 8:31–38) But they can be sure also that Jesus will be there to serve as the leader who gives them strength. "Mark has assured his readers that Jesus will respond generously to their faith in him (2:5) because he has come for the needy (2:17) as a merciful Lord of the Sabbath (2:27 & 564 3:4–5)" (Van Linden, 1989, CBC, p. 911).

VII. PHASE THREE OF THE EXERCISES: WEEKS 17 TO 19

A. Week 17: Jesus is Betrayed

The events of this week that are to be the subject of contemplation enable the exercitants to place themselves with Christ as he suffers in today's world. These events include the Last Supper of Jesus with his disciples, his leave-taking meal **[190–197]**; and his agony and betrayal in the Garden **[200–203]**. Emphasize with the exercitants that these contemplations are meant to give depth to, and to stabilize and strengthen the election made in Phase Two. This is the purpose also of the new guidelines that Ignatius provided for Phase Three **[195, 196, 197]**. And, this is an opportunity also for the exercitants to overcome the all too common revulsion at the prospect of an "on screen" look directly at the bloody, cruel, and apparently useless facts of the Passion and Death of Christ. By confronting these negative impulses straight on, each exercitant may become free enough to immerse totally in the agony and the promise of these events without becoming heartsick and enervated.

PMWYS pp. 123–29

1. *"Consider How The Divinity Hides Itself".*

"The exercitant should give special attention to 'what Christ our Lord suffers in His humanity or wills to suffer' **[195]**, asking for sorrow, affliction, and confusion because the Lord is going to his passion on account of [the exercitant's] sins **[193]**. Special consideration must also be given to how the Divinity hides Itself . . . how It leaves the most Sacred Humanity to suffer so cruelly **[196]**. Again, you, as director, can emphasize that the exercitant should now be able to ask: 'What ought I do for Christ?'" (Egan, 1987, p. 104).

2. *Each Exercitant seeks a "felt knowledge" of Jesus Christ.*

A book on aerobic exercises will produce few beneficial results for one's well being if the exercitant does not stretch her muscles and do the exercises. So too the Spiritual Exercises are meant to be spiritual "aerobics"—exercises to be engaged in, undergone, and deeply experienced. In fact these exercises are not just meditations and contemplations on the mysteries of Jesus' life, death, and resurrection. "They are a method of freeing exercitants of inordinate attachments so that they may more easily find God's specific will for them. . . . Hence Ignatius plunges the exercitant into the mysteries of Christ's life, death, and resurrection, but within the context of specifically Ignatian exercises. . . . The Ignatian "method" initiates the exercitant in the inner logic and dynamism of the Spiritual Exercises, that is into Christocentric consolations and desolations that lead to discernment, decision, and confirmation" (Egan, 1987, p. 105).

3. "Taste" and "See" with the imagination.

During this week there is an "Application of the Senses" exercise **[123–126]** in which the exercitant is directed to see, hear, touch, taste, and smell in his imagination certain features of the mystery being contemplated. Quoted by Rahner, a commentary made by Origen (about 254 A.D.) may give some insight into what Ignatius had in mind thirteen centuries later when he developed his powerful method for using the whole of our sensibility in prayer.

Origen explained: "Christ is the source, and streams of living water flow out of him. He is bread and gives life. And thus he is also spikenard and gives forth fragrance, ointment that turns us into the anointed (christoi). He is something for each particular sense of the soul. He is called Light so that the soul may have eyes. Word, so that it may have ears to hear. Bread, so that it may savour him. Oil of anointing, so that it may breathe in the fragrance of the Word. And he has become flesh, so that the inward hand of the soul may be able to touch something of the Word of life, which fashions itself to correspond with the various manifestations of prayer and which leaves no sense of the soul untouched by his grace" (Rahner, 1968, p. 200).

B. Week 18: Jesus Suffers Injustice, Insults, and Torture

In this week's contemplations, following Ignatius' guidance and the sequence of events in the gospel narratives, we walk with Jesus during his Passion, at first briskly and then more and more slowly: from the Garden of Olives to the house of Annas **[208, 291]**; from the house of Annas to the house of Caiphas **[208, 292]**; from the house of Caiphas to the house of Pilate **[208, 293]**; from the house of Pilate to the house of Herod **[294]**; and finally from the house of Herod back to the house of Pilate again **[208, 295]**. In sum, we place ourselves in this degrading runaround with Jesus as he suffers.

PMWYS *pp. 130–33*

There is probably no ignominy that a human being can suffer that is psychologically and physically worse than being subjected to deliberate injustice, insults, and torture **[291–295]**. Yet the members of Jesus' mystical body continue to live out the excruciating passion and death of Christ in many parts of the world, as worldwide news reporting makes abundantly clear. Fleming summarizes Ignatius commentary pointedly by the highly charged phrase "Jesus lives his passion." It may truly be said today in all too many parts of the world, "Men, women, and children live His passion," but many, if not most, may be unaware of how to transform their passion into the saving passion of Jesus. However, we may confidently believe that he who was able to assure his followers that he could transform the crushed grains of wheat and the bleeding grapes into his life-giving body and blood, just as surely must salvifically transform the injustice, suffering, and death of his brothers and sisters.

WEEK 19: THE KING MOUNTS HIS THRONE OF GLORY

At this point you will want to urge the exercitants not only to vividly picture the events of Christ's passion but also to vividly picture comparable events in the life of those who are members of his mystical body. What is the appropriate response? Empathy alone, the exercitants will see, is not completely authentic living. What is the effective antidote to injustice? to insults? to torture? Guide them to know and hear the answers: respect and love and self-sacrificial kindness.

C. *Week 19: The King Mounts His Throne of Glory*

You, the director, and the exercitants will now ask the Father to place us each somehow with Christ crucified in today's world since he continues to work to save all of us. The meditations of this week focus on Jesus as he is handed over by Pilate to be butchered as the "Lamb of God" (Jn 1: 29, 36) of the New Covenant **[208, 296]**, on Jesus as he dies on the Cross **[208, 297]**, and from the Cross to the Sepulchre **[208, 298]**.

PMWYS* *pp. 134–41

1. The Passion is the Glory of Jesus.

You will recall that unlike the three Synoptics, the fourth gospel reports and considers the Passion of Jesus as "glory" (Jn 19:13–22). An effective approach to these solemn mysteries is for the exercitants to colloquy with Mary. This way each exercitant talks with the Mother of Jesus and asks her to help share "her understanding of, and her way of coming to accept, the sufferings of Jesus' Passion and his "glory."

PMWYS* *p. 135

This "Passion and glory" emphasis is further explained by Harvey Egan. He says "that the *Spiritual Exercises* are an unusually powerful method of simplifying and deepening prayer by way of a gradual interiorization of the mysteries of the life, death, and resurrection of Jesus Christ." Nowhere is this more true than deep within the innermost self of the exercitant in Phase Three. Egan elaborates on this: "This method initiates a twofold process. First, the exercitant becomes connatural with the mysteries of Christ's life, death, and resurrection by assimilating them in much the same way that a student assimilates a book or a great work of art, that is, by internalizing something external. Second, the *Exercises* initiate a movement from the inside to the outside, that is, from the exercitant's core to more exterior levels of his or her being.

2. God—the Mystery who haunts, illuminates, and loves us. Contemporary theology stresses that God communicates himself as the mystery who haunts, illuminates, and loves us at the very roots of our being, even before we begin to seek him. In fact, God's loving word of wisdom at the center of our being sets in motion any genuine search for him.". . . Ignatius uses the outer word of salvation history to awaken, deepen, and set in motion the inner word of God's universal self-communication" (Egan, 1987, pp. 108–109).

VIII. PREPARATION FOR PHASE FOUR PRAYER

"Preparation for Phase Four Prayer" sets the tone of joy and happiness that all exercitants in the group as well as the director should now experience because of the realization that Jesus, who has atoned for our sins, still loves us. Moreover, he is the pledge of our own resurrection to eternal life. Consequently, the gift we beg for now as we prepare for this phase of the Exercises is "The consolation, the joy, the new surge of life that the Risen Christ bestows upon His followers from Easter morning until this present day." Exercitants who absorb the spirit of Jesus in the first three phases of the Exercises should find unsuppressible joy and imperturbable peace of mind and be solidly confirmed in this happiness on completing Phase Four.

PMWYS p. 139

St. Paul expresses it perfectly: "If Jesus be for us, who can be against us?" If our sins are atoned for, if Jesus loves us, if we participate in the life of the Trinity, if Jesus has risen from the dead and is the pledge of our own resurrection to eternal life, what else matters in life, except that we try to give back to God our thanks, praise, and work that his kingdom may come.

A. Phase Four of the Exercises: Weeks 20 to 24 "And hope diffuses through tormented earth."

1. Faith Insight into the "Why" of Christian optimism.

Ignatius proposes for our contemplation thirteen post-resurrection appearances of "the risen Christ" Jesus **[218–229, 299–311]**. In order to best achieve a frame of mind most conducive to reaping the fruits of Phase Four, Ignatius recommends that the first three points be the same as in previous phases. However, as a fourth point he advises the exercitant "to consider how the Divinity, which seemed to hide itself in the Passion, now appears and shows itself so marvelously in the most holy Resurrection by Its true and most holy effects" **[223]**. In the fifth point, Ignatius advises the exercitant "to realize that the role of consoler which Christ performs in each of his resurrection appearances is the same role he performs now in my life" **[224]**. It is this insight based on faith that gives the exercitant the daily assurance that he can live his life with Christian optimism, in spite of the big and little "torments" of everyday living.

PMWYS p. 140

PREPARATION FOR PHASE FOUR PRAYER

2. The Fourfold Colloquy—Its Importance.

In all of the contemplations of Phase Four special attention is to be given to the fourfold colloquy that will spring up spontaneously if the exercitant feels deeply grateful for all of the many gifts bestowed gratuitously **[225M].***

3. Stress Flexibility in Prayer as Ignatius Did.

Ignatius suggests that in Phase Four the mysteries of the Resurrection through the Ascension may be shortened or lengthened by either a selection among, or a division of, the various mysteries. Just as in Phase Three, Ignatius recommends that exercitants be free to engage in those repetitions and application of the senses that most help them **[226]**. It seems quite in keeping with the atmosphere of relaxed consolation in Phase Four to have no more than four or five formal periods of prayer within the week, of which the contemplations of the fourth and fifth days center on aspects of the preceding contemplations that moved the exercitant in special ways **[227M]**. The reason for this flexibility is certainly not because the subject matter of Phase Four is less important than that of earlier phases. Presumably by this stage of the *Exercises*, the exercitant will more readily be able to find God in all things; scriptural passages will provide a focus **[228]** and the gratitude and joy in the remembrance of God's gifts will, will make contemplation easier even if it may be less formalized. Moreover, habits of self denial and self control cultivated in preceding weeks will be strong enough that the exercitant will not take the easy course and "slack off."

PMWYS* *p. 140

4. Reinforce the Atmosphere of Consolation.

Throughout this Phase, you as director should encourage all exercitants to cultivate an innermost atmosphere of happiness, joy and peace. To be genuine this mood must be based on a deeply felt realization of being loved by God who has lavished gifts so great that the exercitant could not have dreamed of asking for them except their existence had been revealed (God sending his Son to atone for our sins by his death; the gift of being welcomed into the family of the Trinity by the sacraments etc.). The beautiful and welcoming environment of the world around us—the sun, light breezes, the beauty of children, the innocence of pets, the fragrance of flowers, and all the rest—should be seen, touched, savored, and cherished in every way. Encourage this exhilaration because it nourishes and reinforces the atmosphere of God's consolation—the knowing that God loves each one because each is special **[229M]**.

PMWYS* *p. 140

* The **M** after any annotation (guideline) number indicates a slight rhetorical modification to the Mullan-Fleming translation.—J.W.S.

B. Week 20: Christ the Lord Conquers Death

WEEK 20: CHRIST THE LORD CONQUERS DEATH

1. Jesus Appears First to His Mother.

An important insight into the sensitive and human face of Ignatian spirituality is the approach that Ignatius makes to the Resurrection of Jesus in Phase Four. The first contemplation proposed to the exercitants is that of Jesus appearing first to console Mary, his mother **[218–219]**. Although there is no scriptural text to literally support the supposition that Jesus first appeared to his mother, Ignatius "understood" with his heart, as we do, that the first person to whom Jesus would return would quite naturally be his mother, the one who had stood by him throughout his Passion and death.

PMWYS *pp. 142–44*

2. "Rejoice and be Glad Intensely" that Christ is Risen.

Ignatius outlines the account in the Scripture narrative of the death and resurrection of Christ **[219]** and then the composition of place at the Sepulchre and at our Lady's home **[220]**. Next he guides the exercitant "to ask for what I want, and it will be here to ask for grace to rejoice and be glad intensely at so great glory and joy of Christ our Lord" **[221]**. "In Ignatius' mind, these two mysteries, the apparition to Mary and the Resurrection, seem to be closely connected" (Cusson, 1988, p. 302). In his Fourth Point for this contemplation, Ignatius quite logically directs us "to consider how the Divinity, which seemed to hide Itself in the Passion, now appears and shows Itself so marvelously in the most holy Resurrection by Its true and most holy effects" **[223]**.

Certainly, the pragmatic mystical insight of Ignatius is captured appealingly in the parallel contemporary rendering of these guidelines **[219–220, 222–224]**. "In contrast to the Passion, I should note how much the divinity shines through the person of Christ in all his appearances. The peace and joy which he wants to share with me can only be a gift of God. To realize that the role of consoler which Christ performs in each of his resurrection appearances is the same role he performs now in my life is a faith insight into why I can live my life in a true christian optimism." (Fleming, 1978, pp. 133 & 35).

Moreover, this is consistent with the two focal points of Ignatian spirituality that are afterwards summarized for Week 24: "the first is that love ought to show itself more in deeds over and above words **[230]**; the second is that love consists in a mutual sharing of goods. For example, a lover gives and shares with the beloved something of his personal gifts or some possession which he has or is able to give; so, too, the beloved shares with the lover. In this way, one who has knowledge shares it

PMWYS *p. 158*

PREPARATION FOR PHASE FOUR PRAYER

with one who does not, and this is true for honors, riches, and so on. In love, one always wants to give to the other" **[231]**.

3. The Marian Mediator Mysticism of Ignatius.

As the author of *Ignatius Loyola the Mystic* has pointed out to us, one can hardly appreciate the richness and warmth of Ignatian spirituality unless one recognizes that his Marian mysticism is "intimately and inextricably associated with Ignatius' Christ-centered mysticism . . . especially his mediator mysticism." (Egan, 1987, pp. 114–18). Egan goes on to cite a number of examples from the *Spiritual Exercises* and other writings that illustrate the importance that Ignatius attached to Mary's intercession. "His (Ignatius') mystical sensitivity to which mediator ought to carry his prayer to the Father or to the Most Holy Trinity, in short, his mediator mysticism, often prompted him to choose Mary for his intercessor" (Egan, 1987, p. 116).

The other very rich and moving contemplations proposed for Week 20 are the appearance of Jesus to Mary Magdalene **[300]** and to the disciples going to Emmaus **[303]**. Both have important layers of meaning for all exercitants since they are reminders of the disciples' lack understanding in spite of having known and experienced Jesus' love so vividly and immediately. But we also see how their sorrow and depression turned into joy when it dawned on them that they had not really absorbed Jesus' full message before his death. Moreover they (and we) are now able to see that Jesus' highest priorities consisted in seeking out and finding them and us to console and sharpen our insight, and consequently our love, joy, and courage.

C. Week 21: The King Sends Forth His Followers, and thus the Risen Lord Shares His Mission

1. Jesus the Consoler—Then and Now.

PMWYS pp. 145–48

Ignatius recommends during this second week of Phase Four that the exercitants contemplate Jesus the Consoler. We are to place ourselves in the mysteries swirling around the reports to the desolate disciples, first that Mary had seen Jesus **[300]**, and then of Jesus' revelation to Thomas of the real meaning of faith **[305]**. In fact, the final chapter of Matthew reports that the two Marys were instructed by the angel to tell the disciples that "he has been raised from the dead and now goes ahead of you to Galilee, where you will see him" (Mt. 28:5–7). Then Jesus the Consoler appeared to them personally, "They hurried away from the tomb half-overjoyed, half-fearful, and ran to carry the good news to his disciples. Suddenly, without warning, Jesus stood before them and said, "Peace!" (Mt. 28:8–9). "The eleven disciples made their way to Galilee, to the mountain to which Jesus had summoned them. At the sight of him, those who had entertained doubts fell down in homage." (Mt. 28:16–17). Then Jesus instructs his disciples to go and make disciples of all nations by baptizing them in the name of the Trinity and teaching them to carry out everything that he had commanded them. The author of the first of the synoptic gospels concludes with the reassurance: "and know that I am with you always, until the end of the world" (Mt. 28:20). It is at that place and on that same occasion that Matthew also reports the missioning of the disciples on the same mountain as that of the Ascension later recounted separately in the Acts of the Apostles. Ignatius makes it clear that the last contemplation of Phase Four ought to be about the Ascension (Acts 1: 1–11; 4) **[226, 312]**.

These contemplations provide a basis for very meaningful discussions, on the significance of the fact that Jesus appeared to the women before he appeared to Peter and the other disciples. The disappointing deportment of the disciples as well as the tragic denials of Jesus by Peter during the Passion, make it abundantly clear that they had really not grasped the message of Jesus. And certainly those failures would have tempted anyone who lacked the clairvoyance of the risen Jesus to reconsider the choice of disciples who were meant to serve as the pillars of his new Church. However, Jesus shows us that he is not only their consoler but ours too and capable of always strengthening frail humans to be effective instruments of the Spirit in their mission to do the work of his Kingdom. What love, consolation and strength that should evoke in each exercitant!

2. Additional Contemplations on Other Appearances of Jesus.

The *Spiritual Exercises* of Ignatius contain points for contemplations on several additional Scriptural texts over and above those already noted. These include the verses in Luke that recount an apparition of Jesus to Peter (Lk 24:9–12, 33–34) **[302]**; the appearance to all the disciples except Thomas (Jn 20: 19–23) **[304]**; the apparition to the seven disciples who had been fishing all night (Jn 21: 1–17) **[306]**; and four other appearances to his disciples (Mt 28:16–20 **[307]**; I Cor 15:6 **[308]**; I Cor 15:7 **[309]**; I Cor 15:8 **[311]**) and an apparition "to Joseph of Arimathea, as is piously meditated and is read in the lives of the Saints" **[310]**.*

* The remark about Joseph of Arimathea exists as a hand-written correction by Ignatius in the Autograph.—J.W.S.

PREPARATION FOR PHASE FOUR PRAYER

D. Week 22. "I will ask the Father and he will give you another Advocate" [Paraclete].

Chapters 14 through 16 of John's Gospel are rich with insights given by Jesus about his Father and the Holy Spirit. The letters of Paul, notably 1 Corinthians 1–11 and Romans 8: 26–27, are some of the other theologically rich writings focused on the Holy Spirit, variously referred to as the Spirit, God's Spirit, and the Spirit of Christ. For reasons related to the religious climate at the time that Ignatius was writing the Spiritual Exercises, and for reasons that I have addressed earlier in this manual, Ignatius could not include explicit contemplations on the Holy Spirit. Nevertheless, because of the centrality of the Holy Spirit in Ignatius' other writings, in New Testament scriptures, as well as a rich literature on the role of the Holy Spirit by modern writers in spirituality, I devote this week of contemplations to the Holy Spirit.

PMWYS *pp. 149–52*

1. The Father knows "what the Spirit means."

Two brief statements in the letter to the Romans explain that the Spirit of God, by dwelling in the baptized, imparts to them the very life of Jesus (Rom 8:26–27). Furthermore, Paul tells us that those who live in the Spirit of Jesus have been freed from sin and death, have their hearts set on spiritual matters, and enjoy peace and life. Then he goes on to develop a most consoling concept regarding prayer: namely that the Spirit, in the one who believes, keeps praying even when the believer does not pray well or does not know how to pray as he ought. The Father, the one "who searches hearts knows what the Spirit means, for the Spirit intercedes for the saints as God himself wills." God the Father, thus, "hears" the Spirit praying in the believer and responds to this perfectly expressed and fully welcomed prayer.

2. Recognize the Holy Spirit as "Creator and Communicator."

Some theologians in recent times have sharpened their focus on an account in *Genesis* of the Spirit as Creator and Communicator. That first role of Creator is, of course, encapsulated magnificently in the phrase "In the beginning, when God created the heavens and the earth . . . a mighty wind swept over the waters" (Gn 1:1). Subsequently, at the Incarnation of Jesus the role of the Holy Spirit is further described: "The Holy Spirit will come upon you and the power of the Most High will overshadow you; hence, the holy offspring to be born will be called Son of

God" (Lk 1:35). The second role as Communicator is attributed to the Holy Spirit because Jesus, the Son of God, is not only the *Word* of God but also the *Image* of God. It is the role of the Spirit to transmit that Word and Image to people of every generation. And as Irenaeus wrote almost eighteen hundred years ago: "Without the Spirit it is impossible to see the Son; without the Son it is impossible to approach the Father." It is a role of communication too that all exercitants, collaborating with the Spirit, carry out in their generation.

E. Week 23: The Prodigal God: The Contemplation on His Unsurpassed Love

PMWYS *pp. 153–57*

One Ignatian scholar thinks that Ignatius seems to have conceived of the Contemplation to Attain Love as an initiation into a life of love, or a pathway to love based on the life and death of Jesus. In another passage the same scholar suggests that "the point of view for the Contemplation to Attain Love is that of the immanence of God in the created world as an expression of his preeminently benevolent love for us." By that is meant that "it is not our knowledge of God which starts *from* the created world, but the knowledge of and the encounter with God *in* creation; for in it God reveals himself essentially as one in a continual act of love for man. Everything is full of the presence and of the love of the Creator for his creature. This awareness of a divine love . . . ignites in the human heart a flame of intense gratitude and of adoration of the eternal Creator and Lord. . . . The Contemplation to Attain Love is simultaneously a respectful attention to finding God present to us in all things and a loving application of one's whole being to serving his Divine Majesty, his Sovereign Goodness" (Cusson, 1988, pp. 317–18).

1. God in All Things—Our Sense of the Cosmic.

Cusson's analysis brings to mind the awe and sense of being in the presence of beauty combined with mystery as one beholds some very beautiful scenes in nature. As a geologist I have been impressed with the close association that exists, for example, between places of great scenic beauty like the National Parks, and their inherent geological interest. What is it that enthralls even those uninitiated in the secrets of geology? What is it in nature that imparts a perception of awe and wonder in those who witness such scenic splendor? The answers are in some ways in the eyes of the beholder. Teilhard de Chardin writes eloquently in several of his essays of this sense of awe and wonder as a Cosmic Sense, a pre-intellectual sense of the cosmic (Teilhard de Chardin, 1950, pp. 17, 21, 40). Moreover, one hopes that the basic human impulse to nature conservancy and environmental protection would be grounded, however inchoately, in beauty and mystery. And the spirituality of Native Americans in its highest form appears to be grounded in a solid perception of the immanence of "the Great Spirit." I believe that a complete spirituality of the Earth and of the Universe will take into account the immanence of God in evolving creation and the divinely designed role for mankind in it. These are precisely the features contained in the *Spiritual Exercises,* especially in the Contemplation to Attain Love.

2. The Focus—God as Both Giver and Gift.

The contemplations of Week 23 are focused on God's gifts to the exercitant **[234]**, on God's gift of himself to the exercitant **[235]**, on God laboring for the exercitant **[236]**, and on God as Giver and Gift. Ignatius suggests that the generous response of the exercitant to such a lavish gift-giver might be summed up in these words **[234]**:

TAKE AND RECEIVE

Take, Lord, and receive all my liberty, my memory, my understanding, and my entire will—all that I have and call my own. You have given it all to me. To you, Lord, I return it. Everything is yours; do with it what you will. Give me only your love and your grace. That is enough for me.

F. Week 24: Totally in His Hands

"The Contemplation for Love is a bridge linking the *Exercises* with the reality of one's everyday life" (Iparraguirre, cited by Stanley, 1986, p. 294). Stanley further elaborates that point by saying "just as the Principle and Foundation **[23]** was a "presupposition for entering into the Spiritual Exercises . . . so this final contemplation assists the exercitant to channel all the newly acquired energies which have graced the retreat into a dynamic living of the gospel."

1. The Focus—Love Expressed in Deeds and in Interchange Between Lover and Loved.

PMWYS pp. 158–61

The first two contemplations of this final week of the Ignatian Retreat focus on two points **[231]**: namely, "that love ought to show itself in deeds over and above words, "and "that love consists in interchange between the two parties," respectively.

The third contemplation, based on **[236]**, guides the exercitant "to consider how God works and labors for me in all things created on the face of the earth . . ." The fourth contemplation, focused on **[237]**, guides the exercitant to reflect "how all the good things and gifts descend from above."

2. And Finally—"Place Me With Your Son!"

The fifth and final contemplation of this Nineteenth Annotation or Ignatian Retreat is a Prayer of Praise that springs from a heart full of gratitude for all of "gifts from above." The generous and daring petition that Ignatius made to Mary to "Place Me With Your Son!" is one to which each exercitant may aspire, having walked the roads and byways with Jesus these many weeks through the mysteries of his life, passion and death, and across the bridge linking the Exercises with the reality of the everyday life to come.

THE EXPEDITION

My retreat has come to an end,
and I think of the days that I have spent
in these surroundings.

I see an image of myself as I was when I came here
and I look at myself as I am today
at the close of the retreat

I think of the persons and places
that have been a part of my retreat.
To each of them I speak in gratitude
and to each I say goodby:
other places, other persons call to me
and I must go.

I think of the experiences I have had,
the graces I have been granted
in this place.
For each of these too I am grateful.

I think of the kind of life I have lived here,
the atmosphere, the daily schedule,
I say goodbye to them:
another type of life awaits me,
other graces, other experiences.

And as I say goodbye to persons,
places,
things,
events,
experiences,
and graces,
I do so under life's imperious bidding:
if I wish to be alive
I must learn to die at every moment,
that is, to say goodbye, let go, move on.

When this is done, I turn to face the future
and I say, "Welcome."

I imagine my trip from this place tomorrow
and I say, "Welcome."

I think of the work that waits for me,
the people I shall meet,
the type of life I shall be living,
the events that will take place tomorrow.
And I extend my arms in welcome
to the summons of the future.

IX. WHAT HAPPENS AFTER THE IGNATIAN RETREAT?

I never cease to be amazed and thrilled that the exercitants are saddened to realize that the retreat is coming to a close. A part of that sadness seems to be due to the source of support, encouragement, and solidarity that the members of the group have been to one another. There is also the question as to whether the exercitant as an individual will be able to take the time consistently to engage in spiritual exercises with a similar intensity in the weeks and months after the retreat. Most of those who enroll in the retreat live busy, even crowded lives, and so this question is a real one, because a very high priority has already had to be placed on spiritual exercises for them to find a place in their normal busy schedules.

1. Recommend that the Exercitants continue the Awareness Examen.

What to do? My first recommendation is that each exercitant, like any "aerobic" brother and sister continue after formal training to exercise in a manner suited to both needs and ongoing constraints. Whatever else may be worked out, the Practice of Awareness Examen (Christian Insight Meditation) should have highest priority. It is a practice of spiritual aerobics that is delightful as well as healthful because gratitude for the gifts of the day is the emotion from which it springs. Moreover, in reflecting on the "gifts from above" the realization comes that one's response falls short of matching the great love of the Creator and Communicator who has given so lavishly. With that realization one is spurred to a healthy renewal of desire to be aware and to labor for the coming of the Kingdom in a way that can somehow reflect the desire of the Spirit who labors for us. Then one ends in either a heartfelt silent or a verbal colloquy. Thus the Awareness Examen is basically a mini-Contemplation to Attain Love.

PMWYS pp. 10–12

2. Recommend also that the Exercitants carry on with Spiritual Direction and Journaling.

A further recommendation is that exercitants continue to consult with and work with a spiritual director so as to develop an ongoing program appropriate to that individual and to life's circumstances. An exercitant who wishes to continue to deepen spiritual awareness and commitment by means of spiritual direction will continue to find that regular journaling will reinforce that activity and provide a means for reflecting on prayer and life experiences. Whatever other specific steps anyone may take to deepen spirituality on a continuing basis, I recommend that the director try to help each interested exercitant consider what avenues may be open and what concrete activities may be appropriate for advancing Christ's Kingdom in the light of the retreat experience. For that a return to the Election may be in order.

REFERENCES CITED

Abbott, Walter M. ed. "Decree on the Apostolate of the Laity" in *The Documents of Vatican II*, pp. 489–521. New York: Guild Press, 1966.

Aschenbrenner, George A. "Consciousness Examen." *Review for Religious*, 31 (1972), pp. 14–21.

Barry, William A. "The Experience of the First and Second Weeks of the Spiritual Exercises." *Review for Religious*, 32. (1973), pp. 102–109.

_______. *Seek My Face: Prayer as Personal Relationship in Scripture*. Mahwah, N.J.: Paulist Press, 1987.

_______. *God and You: Prayer as a Personal Relationship*. Mahwah, N.J.: Paulist Press, 1987.

_______. *Discernment in Prayer: Paying Attention to God*. Notre Dame: Ave Maria Press, 1989.

_______. *Now Choose Life: Conversion as the Way to Life*. Mahwah, N.J.: Paulist Press, 1990.

_______. *Spiritual Direction & the Encounter with God: A Theological Inquiry*. Mahwah, N.J.: Paulist Press, 1992.

_______, 1991. "Founding a Relationship With God." *America*, December 14, pp. 458–62.

_______. *Unpublished Occasional Letters on Ignatian Spirituality #4*, March 9, 1992, p. 1.

Barry, William A. and Connolly, William J. *The Practice of Spiritual Direction*. San Francisco: Harper-Collins, 1981.

Buechner, Frederick. *The Sacred Journey*. San Francisco: Harper & Row, 1982.

Carr, Anne E. *Transforming Grace: Christian Tradition and Women's Experience*. San Francisco: Harper & Row, 1988.

Cowan, Marian, and Futrell, John. *The Spiritual Exercises of St. Ignatius of Loyola: A Handbook for Directors*. New York: Le Jacq, 1982.

Cusson, Gilles, *Biblical Theology and The Spiritual Exercises*; translated from the French by Mary Angela Roduit and George E. Ganss. St. Louis: The Institute of Jesuit Sources, 1988.

_______. *The Spiritual Exercises Made in Everyday Life: A Method and a Biblical Interpretation*. St. Louis: The Institute of Jesuit Sources, 1989.

de Mello, Anthony, *Sadhana: A Way to God. Christian Exercises in Eastern Form*. St. Louis: The Institute of Jesuit Sources, 1978.

_______. *Wellsprings: A Book of Spiritual Exercises*. New York: Image-Books, 1986.

Egan, Harvey D. *The Spiritual Exercises and the Ignatian Mystical Horizon*. St. Louis: The Institute of Jesuit Sources, 1976.

_______. *What are they saying about Mysticism?* Mahwah, N.J.: Paulist Press, 1982.

_______. *Ignatius Loyola the Mystic*, Vol. 5 in The Way of the Christian Mystics series. Wilmington, Del.: Michael Glazier, 1987.

English, John. *Spiritual Freedom: From an Experience of the Ignatian Exercises to the Art of Spiritual Direction*. Guelph, Ontario: Loyola House, 1973.

REFERENCES CITED

Flanagan, Neal M. "John" in *The Collegeville Bible Commentary,* pp. 981–1020. Collegeville, Minn.: The Liturgical Press, 1989.

Fleming, David L. *The Spiritual Exercises of St. Ignatius. A Literal Translation and A Contemporary Reading*. St. Louis: The Institute of Jesuit Sources, 2nd ed. rev., 1980.

______. "The Ignatian Spiritual Exercises: Understanding a Dynamic," pp. 2–18, in Notes on the Spiritual Exercises of St. Ignatius of Loyola, *Review for Religious,* 1983.

Ganss, George E. *The Spiritual Exercises of Saint Ignatius: A Translation and Commentary.* Chicago: Loyola University Press, 1992.

Green, Thomas H. *Weeds Among the Wheat. Discernment: Where Prayer and Action Meet*. Notre Dame: Ave Maria Press, 1984.

Hedberg, Augustin. *Faith Under Fire & the Revolutions in Eastern Europe*. Princeton, N.J.: Sturges, 1992.

Hughes, Gerard W. *The God of Surprises*. London: Darton, Longman and Todd, 1985.

Kodell, Jerome. "Luke" in *The Collegeville Bible Commentary,* 1989, p. 938. Collegeville, Minn.: The Liturgical Press.

Lewis, C. S. *The Screwtape Letters,* 1942 (reprint, New York: Macmillan, 1961).

Peters, William A. M. *The Spiritual Exercises of St. Ignatius: Exposition and Interpretation*. 2nd ed., Rome: Centrum Ignatianum Spiritualitatis, 1978.

Rahner, Hugo. *Ignatius the Theologian;* translated from the German by Michael Barry. New York: Herder & Herder, 1968.

Skehan, James W. *Place Me With Your Son: Ignatian Spirituality in Everyday Life,* 3rd ed. Washington, D.C.: Georgetown University Press, 1991.

Stanley, David M. *"I Encountered God!" The Spiritual Exercises with the Gospel of Saint John*. St. Louis: The Institute of Jesuit Sources, 1986.

Teilhard, de Chardin, Pierre, *The Divine Milieu*. New York: Harper & Row, 1960.

______. *The Heart of Matter;* translated from the French by René Hague. New York: Harcourt Brace Jovanovich, 1979.

Tetlow, Joseph. *Choosing Christ in the World: Directing the Spiritual Exercises of St. Ignatius Loyola According to Annotations Eighteen and Nineteen, A Handbook*. St. Louis: The Institute of Jesuit Sources, 1989.

Toner, Jules J. *Discerning God's Will: Ignatius of Loyola's Teaching on Christian Decision Making*. St. Louis: The Institute of Jesuit Sources, 1991.

Van Linden, Philip, "Mark" in *The Collegeville Bible Commentary,* pp. 903–935. Collegeville, Minn.: The Liturgical Press, 1989.

Forsan et haec olim meminisse juvabit!

The Aeneid / VIRGIL

NOTES

NOTES

ISBN 978-0-87840-569-5